MATTHEW

Catholicos of All the Armenians, 1858–1865
Armenian Patriarch of Constantinople, 1844–1848

The Armenian Awakening

A History of the Armenian
Church, 1820-1860

BY

LEON ARPEE

CHICAGO: THE UNIVERSITY OF CHICAGO PRESS
LONDON: T. FISHER UNWIN, 1 ADELPHI TERRACE
1909

Composed and Printed By
The University of Chicago Press
Chicago, Illinois, U. S. A.

PREFACE

When the history of the regeneration of Turkey is written, a large place will be given to the Armenians of that empire. The Armenians were Turkey's pioneers of enlightenment and civil and religious liberty. In view of this fact, those who have been following recent developments in the Turkish empire will read these pages on the Armenian awakening with special interest.

The fifth and eighth chapters are reproduced in somewhat altered form from the *American Journal of Theology* for April, 1906, and April, 1907, respectively.

The writer desires here to acknowledge the courtesy of the Department of State at Washington, D. C., in transmitting to him a copy of an unpublished diplomatic correspondence on the subject of the treaty rights of American missionaries in Turkey, of which two extracts are given in this book, and of the Protestant Chancery at Constantinople, Turkey, in permitting him to consult the archives of that office for some facts of the early organization of the Protestant civil community in the Turkish empire which could not otherwise have been learned.

CONTENTS

CHAPTER I

CHAPTER II

CHAPTER III

CHAPTER IV

CHAPTER V

A Relic of Primitive Christian Thought—Theology of
the *Key* Unitarian of the Monarchian Type—The *Key*
Teaches That Christ Was Not Endowed with Divine
Powers and Prerogatives Until His Baptism—Pauli-
cians Practice Adult Baptism Exclusively—Paulician
Conception of Baptism and the *Key's* Corresponding
Ritual—Mode of Baptism—Ordination: The Pauli-
cian Ministry not a Priesthood—Sacraments—The
Paulician Canon—"The Universal and Apostolic
Church"—Polity of the · Paulician Church—Pauli-
cianism the Precursor of Protestantism in Europe—
Bread upon the Waters

CHAPTER VI

The First Two Protestant Missionary Societies to
Enter the Turkish Empire—Early Experience of
Pioneer Missionaries of the American Board with the
Armenians of Turkey—Suspension of the Syrian Mis-
sion and Commencement of the Armenian—Armenian
Press at Malta—Missionary Conference at Malta—
Goodell the First Resident American Missionary at
Constantinople—Sahakian—The Mission High School
at Pera—Sahakian in the Parish School at Hasskeuy—
Retrospect—The Imperial Architects, Chief Persecu-
tors—Persecution of 1839—Attitude of the Foreign
Diplomatic Representatives at the Porte—Sudden
Collapse of the Persecution—Gregory Peshtimaljian—
Beginnings of the Evangelical Movement in Nicomedia

CHAPTER VII

Redoubled Efforts—A Revival of Persecuting Zeal and
a Hopeful Outlook—Accession of the Patriarch Matthew: Gathering Clouds—Missionary Activity of the
Evangelicals—The Great Heresiarchs: Goodell's Declaration—Controversy, Private and Public—The Reformers a Small Band—Horatio Southgate—The Hand

CHAPTER VIII

CHAPTER IX

Patriarchate of Constantinople—Oligarchy of the Amiras: Two Warring Factions—The National College at Scutari—The Council of Twenty-four: Their Appointment and Resignation—The Hatti-Sherif of Gulhané—The People Aroused—Appeal to the Sultan: Unsatisfactory Results—Continued Agitation: Appointment of the Twenty-seven and Triumph of the Popular Party—The Twenty-seven Resign and Their Charter Is Destroyed—Conciliatory Policy of Matthew—Dispute between Patriarch and Sarrafs: The Ecclesiastical Council and the Civil Council—The Hatti-Humayoun—The Armenian Constitution of 1860—Obstacles in the Way of Its Enforcement—Results of the Constitution of 1860

CHAPTER I

INTRODUCTION

To the southward of the Caucasus ranges, between the Black and Caspian seas, lies the mountainous plateau in and about which the great rivers of western Asia, the Euphrates and the Tigris, the Araxes and the Koor, take their rise. This region is known to history by the name of Armenia. Ancient Armenia seldom was under a strong centralized government, and therefore seldom had well-defined boundaries. During the period of its greatest territorial extent it reached from 37 to 49 degrees east longitude, and from $37\frac{1}{2}$ to $41\frac{3}{4}$ degrees north latitude. The Armenians appear on the scene of history for the first time about the sixth century before Christ. Prior to their coming there was about Lake Van a kingdom known to the ancient Hebrews as Ararat, and to the Assyrians as Urardhu, inhabited by a people of uncertain ethnological origin. At the time indicated the Armenians, an Aryan people, invaded Ararat and the adjoining territory, and drove out or assimilated the original inhabitants, and gave their name and language to the country.

Christianity very early reached this people. Tradition represents the apostles Thaddeus and Bartholomew as laboring among them; so that while the Greek church prides itself on its orthodoxy, and the Roman church on its catholicity, the Armenian

church prides itself on its apostolicity.   The witness
of tradition to the early origin of Armenian Christianity is confirmed by historical evidence.   According to Tertullian,[1] "the people of the name of Christ"
were found in Armenia in the first half of the third
century, and Eusebius bears witness to the existence
of "brethren" in Armenia in the middle of the same
century, and mentions their bishop, Meroujan, by
name.[2]   What form early Armenian Christianity
assumed is largely a matter for conjecture.   It may
be taken for granted, however, that it was not of
the Byzantine type which we find prevalent in Armenia in the fifth century and onward.

According to the Armenian historians, Gregory
the Illuminator was the founder of Armenian Christianity.   That is, under his labors Christianity was
made by royal edict the established religion of Armenia, and was embraced by the people by wholesale
baptisms.   This was not later than the beginning
of the fourth century.   The Armenian or Gregorian
church, as it is sometimes called after the Illuminator,
therefore, was the first national Christian church
of the world.

The church of Armenia early felt the influence of
Graeco-Roman Christianity.   For some time before
the end of the third quarter of the fourth century
the Armenian catholici or general bishops received
ordination from the metropolitans of Cesarea in

---

[1] *An Answer to the Jews*, chap. vii.

[2] *Church History*, Book VI, chap. xlvi.

Cappadocia. During this period of Graeco-Roman ecclesiastical domination commenced a hellenizing movement in the Armenian church of which the first noted exponent was the "reforming" catholicos Nerses the Great. During the first half of the fifth century, under the catholicos Isaac, and the monk Mesrop, the inventor of the Armenian alphabet, this movement reached its climax. For these two men founded a school of letters, hellenistic in type, to which the Armenians owe the Golden Age of their literature and the "Queen of Versions," as their Bible has been termed by LaCroze, and which did more than any other movement to disseminate hellenistic ideas among the Armenian people. It is not surprising, therefore, that the present national church of the Armenians should resemble, as it does, in all essential particulars, the Greek church.

The general features of Armenian Christianity may be briefly summarized.

The Armenian hierarchy consists of three grades of clergy, namely, (1) bishops, including the catholici, patriarchs, and diocesan bishops, all of whom are celibate; (2) priests, including the parish priests, who must be married before ordination, but are not allowed to remarry, and an order of celibate preachers called *vartabeds* or doctors; and (3) deacons, including, along with deacons proper, sub-deacons, candle-lighters, exorcists, readers, and porters. Its head is the catholicos of Etschmiadzin in Russian Armenia. The prerogatives of this dignitary as

head of the entire Armenian church involve the sole
right to ordain bishops and to consecrate the *muron*
or holy ointment used in various ceremonies of the
church. The administrative powers of his see,
vested since 1808 in a synod over which he presides,
do not extend over Turkish territory.[1]

The Armenians, like the Greeks and Latins, have
seven sacraments. Baptism is administered to
infants eight days old by threefold immersion, with
the adjuncts of confirmation and unction. Baptism
is regarded as the cause of regeneration, and is supposed to remove original sin. It is held to be literally a christening. Without it the infant is a heathen;
and an Armenian mother will not kiss her babe until
it has been baptized. The Armenians celebrate
mass as a propitiatory sacrifice. They believe in
transubstantiation, and venerate the elements as
the divine body and blood. Like the Latin church
and unlike the Greek, they use unleavened bread
in the eucharist, and unlike either mix no water with
the wine. Prayers for the dead accompany the mass,
but no purgatory is recognized. Oricular confession
is observed preparatory to the communion, the priest
imposing penance and pronouncing absolution.

[1] The supreme head of the Armenian church has resided con-
tinuously at Etschmiadzin since the year 1441. There are two
catholicates which are local in their jurisdiction, viz., the catholicate of Aghtamar, on an island of the same name in Lake Van,
established by a schismatic bishop in 1113, and the catholicate
of Sis in Cilicia which dates its existence back to the removal
of the supreme pontifical seat to that city in 1294.

Prayers to the Virgin "Mother of God" and to the saints, and faith in their mediation, and a strict observance of feast-days and fast-days have always been notable features of Armenian orthodoxy. The Armenian calendar contains some variations from the Greek and Latin calendars, chief among which is the joint celebration of Christmas and Epiphany on the 6th day of January, old style.

Armenian doctrine requires special notice. The Armenians, with the Greeks, affirm the procession of the Spirit from the Father alone, while they maintain, against both Greek and Latin orthodoxy, the doctrine of "one nature" in Christ, and reciting the Trisagion with Peter the Fuller's addition, thus, "Holy God, holy and mighty, holy and immortal, *who wast crucified for us*, have mercy upon us," lay themselves open to the charge of Theopaschitism.

The monophysite or *one-nature* teaching of the Armenian church identifies it with the schismatic churches. It is an open question, and one of minor importance, whether or not the Armenians officially participated in the Council of Chalcedon (451) which defined the orthodox doctrine of the person of Christ. But it is a matter of history that in the year 491 they adopted the emperor Zeno's *Henoticon* (482)—a formula of concord which, while condemning both Nestorianism and Eutychianism, assumed a noncommittal attitude toward the decisions of Chalcedon—and consequently were left without the pale of Catholic Christendom when in 519 Latins and Greeks united in rejecting its position. The Henoticon, however, well accorded with the sentiments of the Armenians on the Chalcedonian controversies. While, as against Eutychianism, they affirmed positively the real and unconfused deity and humanity of our Lord, they looked with suspicion on any doctrine of "two natures" as a dangerous approach to Nestorianism. In 596 the Armenians definitively pronounced against the Fourth Ecumenical Council, and excluded from their communion the Iberians (Georgians) of their northern border who had recently adopted its decisions.

If we seek for the reason for the defection of the Armenian church, we shall find it in a twofold difficulty: (1) Verbal. The Armenian word for "nature," *pnoutioun*, etymologically meant "essence," and was employed by the Armenian church fathers as an equivalent not only of the Greek *physis* of ordinary usage which means "nature," but also of Cyril's *physis*, "being" or "existence" (used in the expression *heposis physikē* in his third anathematism against Nestorius), and of the Nicene *ousia*, "substance," as in the equivalent of *homoousion*, *i-pnoutênê*, in the Armenian version of the Nicene Creed.[1] The term "two natures," therefore, con-

1 The Greek οὐσία suffers a similarly ambiguous usage in the very symbol of Chalcedon—ὁμοούσιον τῷ πατρὶ κατὰ τὴν θεότητα, καὶ ὁμοούσιον τὸν αὐτὸν ἡμῖν κατὰ τὴν ἀνθρωπότητα, "consubstantial with the Father according to the Godhead and consubstantial with us according to the manhood," where the first ὁμοούσιον means "of the same substance," the second, "of the same nature."

veyed to the Armenians a suggestion of two several essences or personalities. (2) Doctrinal. The Nicene Creed had declared Christ to be *very God;* and the Armenians could not conceive how one could declare a being possessing a divine personality also to possess a human nature co-ordinate with his deity without thereby predicating a separate personality of the humanity. The use of the designation *Theotokos* or "Mother of God" as applied to the Virgin Mary, adopted by the Armenians with the Council of Ephesus (431) which condemned Nestorius' doctrine of a double personality, further tended to confirm the view that Christ's essential being or personality belonged to his Godhead alone, and that his humanity must be regarded as only an accident of his deity. Thus whether we look at the verbal or at the doctrinal phase of the matter, the Council of Chalcedon, in affirming a doctrine of *two natures* in Christ, appeared to the Armenians to revive the Nestorian heresy.[1]

[1] The following words from a work published in 1874 and bearing the *imprimatur* of the Armenian patriarch of Constantinople and his synod may perhaps be regarded as representing the position of most modern Armenian churchmen on the Chalcedonian controversy: "His [i. e., Nestorius'] followers, on account of their holding to the accidental conjunction of two separate natures [in Christ], were called *diophysites;* and it is these and their like that we anathematize in the order of service laid down by our ritual for the rite of ordination, saying, 'I anathematize all schismatics, namely, Arius, Macedon, Nestorius, and all the train of *diophysites,*' and not those who with orthodox intent hold to the union in Christ of two natures without mixture, with-

Ever since the eleventh century Armenia has been under foreign rule. An Asiatic Poland, it is now divided between the three great empires of the Sultan, the Tzar, and the Shah, and the Armenians are scattered to the four ends of the earth. The history of the dispersion of the Armenians is written in blood. The invasions of Armenia by the savage hordes of Seljoukian Turks began in the first quarter of the eleventh century, and before the end of that century the last of the petty Armenian kingdoms of any importance east of the Anti-Taurus ranges fell (1064). The so-called Tartar invasions followed the Seljoukian early in the second quarter of the thirteenth century, culminating in the barbarities of the bloody Tamerlane who on the eve of the fifteenth century reduced Armenia to one vast charnel-house from Van to Kars. Then followed the devastating rivalries of Persians and Ottoman Turks on Armenian soil lasting for three hundred years and until the middle of the eighteenth century. During

out confusion, and without separation. . . . . Many of the ancient fathers for long years waged long controversies over the term *pnoutioun*. Some meant to convey by the term *pnoutioun* the idea of personal distinctions or *personality*, and hence affirmed that after the union of two natures in Christ there was but one *pnoutioun*, and not two, whilst others affirmed two *pnoutiouns* in Christ, meaning by the term *pnoutioun*, 'nature.' But in later times, when the term *pnoutioun* was defined, all voices became unanimous and all controversies and animosities ceased, and to-day all churches are of like mind in this matter."—Sargisian, *Critical Dogmatics*, pp. 194, 199. For the Armenian Confession see Appendix I.

those centuries when Armenia was constantly trampled by invading hordes, multitudes of its native population emigrated to escape the sword, or were deported by the foreign invader, until only a fraction of the Armenians remained in their ancient home.[1]   Many crossed the Anti-Taurus ranges into Asia Minor— 400,000 in one year (1021) alone—one part of this tide of emigration giving rise to the Armenian principality, later kingdom, of Cilicia on the Mediterranean coast, which had a more or less independent existence from 1080 to 1375.   Others at various times moved northward into Astrakhan, and eastward into Persia, or crossed the seas to the Crimea, to Moldavia, to Poland, and to Italy.   Over 40,000 families emigrated to Poland alone, and in the years 1605 and 1608 Shah Abbas I deported 25,000 Armenian families to Persia, whence in course of time

[1] The population of the Armenian table-land before the massacres of 1895 is estimated by a recent writer as follows: Armenians, 906,984; Turks, 489,931; Kurds, 479,676; Tartars, 306,310; Greeks, 52,367; Russians, 28,844; Others, 84,439; Total, 2,348,551. The same writer gives the figures for the Armenian dispersion as follows: Caucasus and remainder of Russian Trans-Caucasia, 450,000; Astrakhan and Bessarabia, 75,600; Remainder of Asiatic Turkey, 751,500; Turkey in Europe, 186,000; Azerbaijan province of Persia, 28,890; Colony of Julfah and remainder of Persia, 14,110; Bulgaria and Eastern Roumelia, 5,010; Roumania, 8,070; Austria, 1,230. He puts the total number of Armenians throughout the world at 3,000,000 (Lynch, *Armenia*, Vol. II, pp. 414, 428). The United States Census Bureau puts the present number of Orthodox Armenians in the United States at about 20,000. Other Armenians in this country would probably swell the total to not less than 25,000.

Armenian colonies found their way to India, China, and the Islands of the Sea.

Through all these vicissitudes of national history the Armenian church remained the only institution of any permanence among the Armenian people. It accompanied them wherever they went, from China to the British Isles, and from Alexandria to St. Petersburg, and proved, the Armenian language and literature not excepted, the most important bond of national unity.   Thus the Armenian church and the Armenian people were more than ever closely identified.

At the time under discussion in the following pages the Armenians were no longer a martial people, but a race of tillers, artisans, traders, and financiers. The great bulk of them dwelt, as they still do, in the Sultan's dominions.   Constantinople was the real center of their ecclesiastical and national life.   The Armenian patriarch of that city, and not the catholicos of Etschmiadzin, was their most important national dignitary.   In the Sultan's capital, he lived in the largest Armenian community in the world; and his civil-ecclesiastical authority made him practically the most powerful official among the Armenians at large.

The Armenian patriarchate of Constantinople, the center of the quasi-feudal system of government under which the Turkish Armenians, as one of the tolerated religious communities of the Ottoman empire, lived, was created by Mohammed II, the

Conqueror, in 1461, when he transferred Joachim, the Armenian bishop of Brousa, to his new capital, and vested him, under the title of "Patriarch," with the supreme civil magistracy in the Armenian "nation" of Turkey; since which date the Armenian patriarch of Constantinople has been bishop of Constantinople and chief magistrate of the Armenians of Turkey at the same time. The office was created solely with a political purpose.[1] The Armenian patriarch of Constantinople represented Turkey's Armenian community at the Porte, and was its recognized head. The Turkish government dealt with its Armenian subjects through the patriarch and his diocesan bishops, who, his ecclesiastical peers, were his civil subordinates. All applications of Armenians for traveling passports and licenses of marriage or burial were received through them, and so was the annual tribute of the community. Until the promulgation of the Hatti-Sherif of 1839, the patriarch and his agents, within limits, possessed penal authority over their people. At the capital the patriarch had his own jail, and maintained a small police force. His authority over his clergy being absolute, he could imprison or exile them at will; and while he was compelled to secure the consent of the Turkish government to imprison or exile laymen of his community, the necessary firman as a

[1] The Armenian patriarchate of Jerusalem, which now is practically only a local bishopric, was originally founded (1311) by the Sultan of Egypt with a similar object.

rule was very easily obtained, especially if the request were reinforced with a bribe. The patriarchal system of government, in placing civil powers in the hands of high ecclesiastics, naturally became a source of much religious oppression, which was only aggravated by the fact that the Porte itself made no distinction between church and community, and often lent the weight of its authority to maintain the integrity of the church, or connived at the oppressive measures of ecclesiastical dignitaries who used their civil powers to persecute heretics and other religious offenders.

If it be asked what the spiritual condition of the Armenian church was at the dawn of the nineteenth century, the answer is not far to seek. Vital religion among the people was at a low ebb. Superstition, ceremonialism, and priestcraft prevailed. The veneration of anointed crosses, of pictures and relics of saints, the giving of alms, the observance of penances, fasts, and vigils, and the going on pilgrimages to Etschmiadzin and Jerusalem, to most Armenians constituted the sum and substance of religion. Preaching in the Armenian church was very uncommon. The parish priests never preached. Most of the preaching was done by vartabeds sent out from Etschmiadzin, Jerusalem, and other monastic centers, with whom it was partly a matter of reciting the virtues of relics and recounting the legends of saints, and largely a matter of appealing for contributions. The Bible was not generally read. One reason for this was that copies of it were not easily obtained. Claudius Buchanan, writing in 1811, stated that copies of the Armenian Bible were very rare in Persia, and in India were scarcely to be purchased at any price.[1] A similar statement, with but slight qualification, would have applied to the Armenian dispersion at large. Prior to the second or third decade of the nineteenth century the introduction of the art of printing among the Armenians was of but little service to the diffusion of the Scriptures among them. Bibles like those printed at Amsterdam (1666–68) and at Venice (1735 and 1805) were intended mainly for the use of the clergy, and were issued at prohibitive prices. It was really the modern Bible and missionary societies that first published Bibles at prices within the means of the common people anywhere. But there was another great obstacle to the general dissemination of the Scriptures among the Armenians, and that was the language of the Armenian Bible. Translated in the first half of the fifth century, the Armenian Scriptures were in the ancient classical tongue, unintelligible to the common people, and often to the priest who conducted the church's services. It was as if modern Italians had no other Scriptures than the Latin Vulgate, or modern Greeks no other Scriptures than the ancient Greek Bible. Hence while it was still the object of a half-superstitious veneration, the Bible was at the beginning of the last century to the great mass of the Armenians a sealed book.

[1] *Christian Researches in Asia*, p. 139.

CHAPTER II

THE REVIVAL OF LEARNING

That period of Armenian church history which
we have called "The Armenian Awakening" follows
close upon three or four centuries which we may
term "The Dark Ages." The foreign invasions of
Armenia and Cilicia left these lands desolate. And
hand in hand with the greatest material desolation
came thick intellectual darkness. When it is recalled
what havoc a Thirty Years' War wrought in the
intellectual life of modern Germany, it will easily
be imagined what centuries of warfare and carnage
must have brought upon the lands just named.
When political conditions allowed—especially in the
fifth and the twelfth century, respectively known as
the Golden and the Silver Age of Armenian literature—the Armenians developed a literature of which
they need not be ashamed. But after the Tartar
invasions of the mother country, and the conquest
of Cilicia by the Egyptian Mamelukes, or from the
end of the fourteenth century onward, literature and
learning on Armenian soil were practically things
of the past. It is the purpose of this chapter briefly
to review the agencies which were slowly at work
during the Dark Ages, with the promise of a new day
for the Armenian race.

Among a people like the Armenians whose literature grew up almost exclusively in monasteries, it

will not seem strange that the revival of learning also should originate in monasteries. The Armenian revival of learning owes its inception mainly to two monastic institutions, namely, the Great Hermitage, and the Convent of Amrdol.

The first was the headquarters of an order of anchorites, founded about the year 1610 by Sergius, formerly abbot of a convent near Erivan, and a priest from Trebizond by the name of Giragos. It was located near Datev, in the mountains of the province of Siunik, in northern Armenia. The order revived the long-forgotten austerities of asceticism among the Armenians. Its rules required obedience, confession, and purity, and imposed community of goods, vigils, fasts, and abstention from meat and wine. But what interests us most is that the members of the order were pledged to cultivate the long-lost art of the reading of books—a requirement by virtue of which the order got itself the name of the School of Siunik. The members of this order not only carried on an extensive ascetical and educational propaganda throughout the country, but instituted a reform movement in the church, and for that reason were persecuted by the corrupt catholicos of the time, Melchizedek.

The second institution named, the Convent of Amrdol, was located at Bitlis, and was made famous by the labors of the Abbot Basil (died, 1615) who revived the old school of the convent, and, what is of special interest, encouraged the pursuit of studies other than strictly theological, namely, grammar and philosophy. Toward the end of the seventeenth century the Abbot Vartan (died, 1705) was noted as an educator at this institution.

To the revival of learning inaugurated by these schools in the first quarter of the seventeenth century we owe three great leaders of education in the Armenian colonies: Hatschadour of Cesarea, bishop of New Julfah, Mekhitar of Sivas, abbot of the Mekhitarist Convent of Venice, and John Golod of Bitlis, Armenian patriarch of Constantinople.

Shah Abbas, who, with barbarous cruelty deported tens of thousands of Armenians into his dominions, and subjected some of their colonies in Persia to untold oppressions, treated the Armenians from Julfah on the Araxes with exceptional favor. These were granted a site two miles to the south of Ispahan, his capital, where they built (1606) the city of New Julfah, and, in the enjoyment of a municipal government of their own coupled with the fullest religious liberty, attained in a short time to a high degree of material prosperity. The merchants of New Julfah carried on a brisk trade with India on the one side, and Russia and the west on the other. The city soon became the center of the wealth of the Armenians of Persia.[1]

---

[1] In 1722 New Julfah fell into the hands of the Afghan invaders, and during the times of anarchy and civil war following the assassination of Nadir Shah (1747) suffered greatly from the depredations of rival khans. As a result large numbers of its

New Julfah had not long been founded when the people built in the city the Convent of the Universal Savior. Hatschadour of Cesarea, the second bishop of New Julfah (1620–46), established here a conventual school, in which, we are told, he taught "all the liberal and the metaphysical arts." Here also, in 1640, he installed a printing-press. Under Hatschadour and his pupil and successor in the episcopal chair, David (1652–83), the school was a noted institution. It served to add to New Julfah's fame as a city of wealth the luster of learning.[1]

Four men who received their training under Hatschadour and David acquired more than a local fame. Simeon of Julfah became noted as an educator, first at Ispahan, and later at Etschmiadzin. Jacob of Julfah became catholicos as Jacob IV. Under his auspices an Armenian printing-office was established at Amsterdam in Holland (1660). Osgan of Ispahan, commonly known as of Erivan, printed at this office a number of Armenian books, among which his Bible deserves special notice as the

inhabitants fled never to return (the Lazarians of Russia, whose family is noted for the founding of the Academy of Oriental Languages of Moscow in 1815, emigrated from New Julfah in the year of Nadir Shah's assassination). At one time a city of 60,000 inhabitants, today it has barely a population of 3,000.

[1] Later in the century we find a large number of the sons of merchants of the city in attendance at this school, learning the rudiments of reading, writing, and arithmetic. Early in the eighteenth century two parish schools were opened in the city for the younger scholars.

first complete printed edition of the Armenian Scriptures (1666–68). John of Julfah fought the Jesuits, and championed the cause of Armenian Christianity against the proselyting projects of Shah Husein (1694–1722), and distinguished himself as a scholar and writer. He made a parallel version of the New Testament into the Persian and Arabic tongues.[1]

Mekhitar was a priest of the Armenian church. In the year 1700 he, with a few followers, came from Erzroom to Constantinople. He took up his residence in the suburb of Galata, and for a while

---

[1] Was this the book to which the traveler Hanway (quoted by Buchanan, *Christian Researches*, pp. 99 f.) in the following century referred when he spoke of "an ancient Arabic and Persian translation" made use of in 1740 in the preparation of a popular Persian translation of the four gospels by Nadir Shah's orders?

We know of two other early translations of the Bible made by Armenian scholars. During the second half of the seventeenth century a translation of the entire New Testament and portions of the Old into Turkish was made by a learned Armenian layman of Constantinople by the name of Keomurjian (cf. Chamchean, *Armenian History*, Vol. III, p. 723), and in 1804 a translation of the entire Scriptures into Chinese was begun by another Armenian layman, Lassarian, who was from the Portuguese port of Macao, China. Lassarian's work was done in India, under the auspices of Claudius Buchanan, vice-provost of the College of Fort William at Calcutta. His translation was published in parts at various intervals, and finally in its entirety in 1822 after being revised from the original languages by his pupil in Chinese, the Baptist missionary Marshman of Serampore (Buchanan, *Christian Researches*, pp. 9 ff.; *The Panoplist*, December, 1812, pp. 289 f.). The Armenian scholars made their translations of the Scriptures from the Armenian Bible.

preached in the Church of Gregory the Illuminator. In 1701 he organized his disciples into a religious order. But presently a persecution of the papal Armenians broke out. Mekhitar and his followers belonged to the Romanist party, and they were compelled to seek safety abroad. In 1703 Mekhitar landed at Modon on the Morea, which was then under the Venetian government. The young priest now organized his order under Benedictine rules, and erected at Modon a monastery of which he was designated abbot by bull of Pope Clement XI (1712). But Mekhitar and his monks were not destined long to remain on the Morea. In 1715, anticipating the Ottoman occupation of the peninsula, the abbot of Modon removed to Venice—a city which from Cilician days had harbored a prosperous colony of Armenians—and in 1717 leased the island of St. Lazarus, on which he founded the convent which still bears his name, and which now for two centuries has been the center of extensive missionary, educational, and literary activity. Mekhitar has left besides some religious writings a number of educational works. His brief grammar of the modern Armenian, published at Venice in 1727, is noteworthy as being the first attempt to familiarize the Armenian people with the laws of their vernacular. Nor is it the least of Mekhitar's achievements that he founded a school of letters which in later times was made illustrious by the labors of such men as Chamchean, the grammarian and historian, Injijian, the geographer and archaeologist, the lexicographers Avedickian, Surmelian, and Avkerian, and the poets Bagratouni and Alishan—men who called forth a new Armenian literature from the ashes of the old.

But for our purpose Constantinople is of greater interest than either New Julfah or Venice.

Armenians began to colonize Constantinople as early as the fifth and sixth centuries of our era. About the beginning of the fourteenth century the Armenians of the Byzantine capital for the first time come under our notice as a distinct ecclesiastical community with a resident bishop. In 1360 we find that they have a church dedicated to St. Sergius. In 1391 an Armenian of Theodosia on the Crimea built in the suburb of Galata the Church of Gregory the Illuminator.[1]

Mohammed II, the Ottoman conqueror, who captured Constantinople in 1453, and peopled the half-depleted capital of the Byzantines with all the races of his newly acquired dominions, gave a new impulse to the influx of Armenians into the city by importing Armenians from Asia Minor and the Crimea, and by establishing in 1461 the Armenian

[1] Armenians played an important part in Byzantine politics. Many of them held high military positions in the empire, and a number of them even ascended the throne of the Caesars. The following emperors were of Armenian birth: Maurice (582–602); Philippicus-Bardanes (711–13); Leo V (813–20); Basil I (867–86), founder of the Macedonian Dynasty; Romanus I (919–44), and John Zimisces (969–76). Cf. Chamchean, *Armenian History*, Vol. II, pp. 1013 f.

patriarchate of Constantinople, which soon became the center of western Armenian life, with the result that by the beginning of the nineteenth century the Armenians of Constantinople came to number upward of 150,000, or not less than one-fifth of the entire population of the city.

All the great popular reform movements in the Armenian church of the last century centered at Constantinople. This is to be explained largely by the fact that popular education had made greater headway among the Armenians of Constantinople than in any other colony of the Armenian dispersion. The father of the new era of enlightenment among the Armenians of the Turkish capital was the progressive patriarch John Golod of Bitlis (1715–41) who founded a seminary in the suburb of Scutari in the early years of his patriarchate. The movement thus inaugurated was fostered by later hands. Golod's pupil and successor, the patriarch Jacob Nalyan (1741–49, 1752–64), founded the patriarchal academy, so famous in the early years of the last century, and thus gave a further impulse to the cause of education among the Armenians of Constantinople. Finally, in the second year of the reign of Sultan Selim III (1789–1807), an Armenian magnate by the name of Schnork Megrditsch established a parochial school in the quarter of Koom-kapou, and this served as a model for similar schools soon established in the parishes of Balat, Ortakeuy, Kouroucheshmé, Psamatia, and Scutari. Thus by the first

half of the last century popular education, though
very elementary and much in need of improvement,
had become a common thing among the Armenians
of the Turkish metropolis, at least so far as the male
portion of the community was concerned.

In reviewing the agencies which made for the
intellectual quickening of the Armenian world during
the Dark Ages, we must not overlook the introduction of the art of printing among the Armenians—
a process of well-nigh three hundred years, which,
while it bore little fruit at the time, was full of the
promise of great things in the future. The first
Armenian books printed appeared at Venice in the
years 1512 and 1513. Between 1565 and 1569, the
Armenian, Abgar of Tocat, an emissary of the catholicos Michael to Pope Pius IV, and others of his
countrymen, printed a number of Armenian books
at Venice and Constantinople. During the seventeenth century more Armenians, some of them independently and some under the auspices of the
catholici, went to Europe, in view of the facilities
there afforded, and published, in various cities of
that continent, a number of Armenian books. Thus
in the course of that century Armenian books were
printed at Lemberg (1616), Venice (1642–), Leghorn
(1643–), Amsterdam (1660–), and Marseilles
(1673–). As the new art was better appreciated,
and as it became increasingly feasible, printing
establishments were founded nearer home, and in
1640 we find an Armenian printing-office established

at New Julfah, then one at Constantinople (1677), another at Smyrna (1759), and still another at Etschmiadzin (1771). The art of printing was well received among the Armenians of the Turkish capital. Between 1677 and 1800 no less than eleven printing establishments are known to have been at different times in operation in that city, some of them through a long period of years.[1]

The agencies above reviewed, in making for the intellectual quickening of the Armenians, at the same time prepared them for a religious awakening. By the beginning of the nineteenth century the Armenians, both clergy and laity, were commencing to show signs of a religious unrest. As early as the year 1760 an Armenian priest residing at Psamatia, Constantinople, by the name of Dibajian, wrote a book to expose the abuses and superstitions of the church. The work was more or less extensively circulated in manuscript as late as the first decades of the last century.[2] And we have it on good authority that in the early years of the nineteenth century there was not a place of importance in the Turkish empire where there were not at least a few Armenians who were aware of the corrupt state of their church

---

[1] It should be stated, however, that when Smith and Dwight visited Constantinople in 1830 they found only one Armenian printing establishment actually in operation in that city, and they were assured that it was at that time the only one in all Turkey (*Researches in Armenia*, Vol. I, p. 67).

[2] See Dwight, *Christianity Revived in the East*, pp. 5 ff.

and eager for its reformation.[1]   As the Renaissance in Europe paved the way for the Reformation, so the revival of learning among the Armenians prepared the way for a new order in the Armenian church.

[1] Prime, *Goodell's Memoirs*, p. 173.

CHAPTER III

POLITICAL HISTORY OF THE PERIOD

Adequately to understand the great nineteenth century movements in the Armenian church, one must needs take into account the history of contemporary European politics as reflected at the Sublime Porte. Without this some of the most important events in the history of those movements would be unintelligible, as the fortunes of the Armenian church often varied only because the balance of international politics inclined one way or the other.

With the disappearance of Napoleon Bonaparte from the scene of European politics, French diplomacy at the Porte assumed a secondary importance, leaving the field of action to the two great rivals, Russia and Great Britain, respectively the natural enemy and the self-interested patron of the Turk. The history of Turkish politics during the period under consideration is distinctly divided into two parts at the year 1833, the first part being marked by the ascendency of Russian influence at the Porte, the second by the ascendency of British influence.

In the thirteenth year of the reign of Sultan Mahmoud II (1808–39) the Greek War of Independence broke out (1821). After a three-years' ineffectual struggle, the Sultan appealed (January 16, 1824) to his vassal, Mehemet Ali Pasha of Egypt, who had risen to power since the expulsion of the French

from that province, and in May, 1825, Ibrahim
Pasha, after reducing Crete, landed his father's
well-disciplined army of Egyptians on the Morea.
But ere long Europe was roused to the fact that
Ibrahim was carrying on a war of extermination;
and the British government sought to bring about an
understanding between the great powers with the
purpose of putting an end to the bloody conflict on
the Greek peninsula. Thus shortly after the fall
of the Acropolis of Athens—the last stronghold of
the Greek revolution—Great Britain, France, and
Russia signed the Treaty of London by which they
bound themselves to cause a cessation of hostilities,
and to secure the practical independence of Greece
from Turkish rule (July 6, 1827). The mediation
of the powers, however, was rejected by the Porte,
and the combined fleets of the allies, under the command of Sir Edward Codrington, appeared before
Navarino, where after a vain effort at negotiation
with Ibrahim, the naval battle was fought in which
the Turkish-Egyptian fleet was all but annihilated
(October 20, 1827).

British statesmen called the battle of Navarino
an "untoward event," and declined to resort to any
further use of force against the Turks. But Russia,
now assured at least of British neutrality in view of
the Treaty of London, was only too eager to appeal
to arms—something which Great Britain had hin-
dered her from doing at the commencement of the
Greek revolution. She made preparations for war

on her borders.   Troops were massed in Bessarabia, and military stores were collected in the harbors of the Black Sea.

The Sultan perceiving these preparations issued a proclamation calling the faithful to arms (December 18).   Russia answered the challenge by a declaration of war in the spring of 1828 (April 26).   Mahmoud had but recently destroyed his old troops, the Janissaries (June 27, 1826), and was able to place in the field only 40,000 modern troops.   It is not surprising, therefore, that the first campaign of the war closed with the Russians in possession of Bucharest and the Black Sea coast as far as Varna, in Europe, and of Toprakkaleh and Diadin in Asia.   The campaign of 1829 brought further disasters to the Turks.   At the battle of Kulevtscha the Russians under the command of Marshal Diebitsch completely routed the enemy.   Then came the surrender of Silistria, which opened the road to Constantinople. The Russian general struck boldly into the enemy's country, and occupied Adrianople, while his vanguard advanced to Kirk-Kilisa on the left, and Enos on the Aegean on the right.   Panic and impending insurrection in his capital left the Sultan no choice but to secure peace almost at any price.   On September 14, 1829, was signed the Treaty of Adrianople. Moldavia and Wallachia thus became practically independent states under Russian protectorate, the Servians were confirmed in their rights of internal self-government, while a part of the left bank of the

lower Danube, and the Asiatic ports of Anapa and
Poti, with the adjoining territory as far as Erivan,
passed under Russian control. In May, 1830, the
Sultan acknowledged the independence of Greece.

But barely had the war with Russia been ended
when Mehemet Ali demanded the reward of his
services in Greece. He had his eye upon Syria; and
as the Sultan refused to surrender to him that province of his empire, he resolved to secure it by force
of arms. His fleet had already been restored since
the day of Navarino, and he was now in possession
of a veteran army under the able generalship of his
son. A pretext for hostilities was found in a dispute
with Abdallah, the pasha of Acre, over some fugitive
fellahs, and in November, 1831, the Egyptian army
was launched into Syria. Acre fell on May 27, 1832.
At Hums in the valley of the Assy (the ancient
Orontes), at the pass of Beylan, near the ancient
Issus, and at Konieh, the ancient Iconium, the armies
of the Sultan were successively defeated, and Ibrahim advanced rapidly westward.

In his extremity Mahmoud sought the help of
Great Britain. But that power was not at that
juncture in a position to meet the emergency, and
the Sultan had to resort to the only other alternative,
that of soliciting the protection of his late foe. Russia seized the opportunity. First one army of six
thousand Russian troops, and then another, was
landed on the banks of the Bosphorus. At sight
of them Ibrahim halted, and terms of peace were

signed at Kutaya (April, 1833), and the empire was
saved from imminent peril; but at great cost to the
Sultan.   By an imperial firman of May 5 Mehemet
Ali was confirmed as pasha of Egypt and Crete, and
was given, besides, the whole of Syria and Adana.
To complete Mahmoud's humiliation, before the
Russian forces were withdrawn from Constantinople
the Sultan was compelled to sign the Treaty of Hunkiar Iskelessi (July 8, 1833) by which he entered
into an offensive and defensive alliance with Russia
and pledged himself to close the Dardanelles in time
of war against the fleets of Russia's foes.

But in exacting this treaty from Turkey, Russia
had overreached herself.   Great Britain was thoroughly aroused by that compact, and set herself to
work in earnest to neutralize the influence of late
years gained by Russia in the Turkish empire.   The
Treaty of Hunkiar Iskelessi thus constituted a turn-
ing-point in the history of Russian and British diplomacy at the Porte.   From 1833 onward British
diplomacy gradually gains the ascendency in
Turkish politics.

A second war of the Sultan with Mehemet Ali
brought Great Britain into active prominence.
Mehemet's ambitions looked toward the establishment of an independent hereditary monarchy over
extensive portions of the Sultan's empire.   With
that end in view he refused to pay tribute to Mahmoud and dismissed the Turkish guards from the
Tomb of the Prophet at Medina.   On June 6, 1839,

the Sultan, who had been preparing for another
struggle in the hope of recovering his lost provinces,
declared war. An army under the command of
Hafiz Pasha, after reducing some Kurdish tribes,
marched against Ibrahim. A splendid fleet of
thirty-six vessels commanded by Ahmed Fevzy sailed
out from the harbor of Constantinople. But both
army and navy were to disappoint all expectations.
On June 24, 1839, the Turkish army, after whole
battalions had deserted to the enemy, met with a
crushing defeat on the plain of Nezib near the city
of Aintab. In the following month (July 13) the
admiral of the fleet, learning of the Sultan's death
(July 1) and of the accession of a personal enemy,
Khosrev Pasha, to power as grand vizier, sailed to
Alexandria and delivered up his entire armament to
Mehemet Ali.

The Ottoman empire was now on the very verge
of ruin. But in its last extremity Great Britain and
France came to its rescue. Their fleets cast anchor
in the Dardanelles, and a series of negotiations
ensued. Finally, on July 15, 1840, Great Britain,
Prussia, Austria, and Russia signed with the Porte
a treaty whereby the Sultan agreed to accord to
Mehemet Ali the life-possession of the Pashalic of
Acre and the hereditary possession of Egypt, provided that he would accept this arrangement within
ten days. As Mehemet refused to acquiesce, a
British and Austrian squadron, under the command
of Sir Charles Napier, proceeded to the Levant.

Beirut was captured in October, and Acre in November. Mehemet Ali agreed at last by a treaty
signed November 27, 1840, to restore the Sultan's
fleet, to evacuate Syria, Arabia, and Crete, and to
renounce all claims except those of hereditary
pasha of Egypt. The Treaty of Hunkiar Iskelessi
was now annulled by a treaty in which Russia
joined with the other powers declaring the Bosphorus and the Dardanelles closed against the
fleets of all foreign nations (July 13, 1841).
Great Britain was the only power that came out
of these negotiations with unqualified cause for
satisfaction.

Scarcely had the young Abdul Medjid (1839–61)
been on the throne four months when he issued an
edict which was hailed as the pledge of a new era
of prosperity for the Turkish empire. This document, the Hatti-Sherif of Gulhané (November 3,
1839), which has been called the Magna Charta of
Ottoman liberties, promised to the subjects of the
Porte a new code of laws guaranteeing security for
life, honor, and property, a regular system of levying
and collecting the taxes, and an equally regular system of recruiting the army and fixing the duration
of the service. The opening paragraphs of this
famous edict will be of interest here:

It is well known that, during the early ages of the Ottoman
monarchy, the glorious precepts of the Koran and the laws of
the empire were ever held in honor. In consequence of this
the empire increased in strength and greatness, and all the

population, without exception, acquired a high degree of welfare and prosperity.

For one hundred and fifty years a succession of incidents and various causes has checked this obedience to the sacred code of the law, and to the regulations which emanate from it, and the previous internal strength and prosperity have been converted into weakness and poverty; for, in truth, an empire loses all its stability when it ceases to observe its laws.

These considerations have been ever present to our mind, and since the day of our accession to the throne the thought of the public good, of the amelioration of the condition of the provinces, and the alleviation of the national burthens, have not ceased to claim our entire attention. If we take into consideration the geographical position of the Ottoman provinces, the fertility of the soil, and the aptness and intelligence of the inhabitants, we shall attain the conviction that, by applying ourselves to discover efficacious methods, the result which, with the aid of God, we hope to obtain, will be realized within a few years.

Thus, then, full of confidence in the help of the Most High, supported by the intercession of our Prophet, we consider it advisable to attempt by new institutions to obtain for the provinces composing the Ottoman empire the benefits of a good administration.[1]

The Sultan, however, was not to be allowed to prosecute his plans of reform unmolested. Russia sought another opportunity to strike a blow. The completed suppression of the national Hungarian government (1849) left the hands of the emperor Nicholas I free to deal with the possessions of what

[1] The full text of this instrument will be found in Creasy, *History of the Ottoman Turks* (ed. of 1858), Vol. II, pp. 452 ff., and in Prime, *Goodell's Memoirs*, pp. 480 ff.

he called the "Sick Man." A dispute between
Latin and Greek Christians over the custody of
some holy places in Palestine, in which the French
emperor had taken up the cause of his coreligionists,
served as the occasion for the reassertion of a long-
standing claim of Russian protectorate over the
Greek Christians of the Ottoman empire, and as
Abdul Medjid refused to admit the claim, a Russian
army, under the command of General Gortschakoff,
invaded the Danubian Principalities (Moldavia and
Wallachia) on July 3, 1853.

War was declared by the Porte on October 4,
1853. Omar Pasha presently took up the offensive,
crossed the Danube, and gained some small victories
over the Russians. Meantime the Turkish fleet
was destroyed in the Black Sea by Admiral Nak-
himoff (November 30, 1853). But Great Britain
and France were not to leave Turkey to fight her
battles alone. On April 10, 1854, these three powers
concluded a treaty of offensive and defensive alliance.
The British and French fleets, which had entered
the Marmora in the preceding September, now
sailed into the Black Sea, and landed an army first
at Gallipoli and then at Varna. Upon the occupation of the Danubian Principalities by Austria and
their evacuation by the Russians, this army set out
on an expedition against the Crimea. For more
than a year that peninsula was the scene of the international conflict. After an eleven-months' siege,
made famous by the battles of Balaclava (October

25) and Inkerman (November 5), Sebastopol was captured by the allies, on September 8, 1855. Finally, on February 25, 1856, the plenipotentiaries of the belligerent powers assembled in the city of Paris, and on March 30 signed a treaty which marked the close of the Crimean War. Thus Russia ceded to Turkey her former acquisitions on the mouth of the Danube, the Black Sea was declared neutral, the Russian protectorate over the Danubian Principalities was annulled, and those provinces as well as Servia were placed under the joint guardianship of the powers.

British statesmen were now beginning to perceive that, all the armed efforts of their government to preserve the integrity of the Ottoman empire notwithstanding, they could never hope to be able to put an end to Russian intrigue and armed aggression in Turkey, unless they removed what had always been made their occasion and excuse, namely, the abuses and corruptions of the internal administration, and the consequent instability of the "decayed empire." They therefore began at this time to encourage all efforts at internal reform in Turkey, regarding such reform as the most effective check to Russian ambition. It was under the direct influence of the famous British ambassador, Lord Stratford de Redcliffe, that on February 21, 1856, Sultan Abdul Medjid published his second decree of internal reform in the empire, the Hatti-Humayoun[1] (recog-

---

[1] See Creasy, *History of the Ottoman Turks*, Vol. II, pp. 456 ff., or Prime, *Goodell's Memoirs*, pp. 486 ff.

nized in the ninth article of the Treaty of Paris), which declared all distinctions between Ottoman subjects on the score of race or creed abolished, and established civil and military equality between Christians and Moslems.

The constitution which Sultan Abdul Hamid II granted to his subjects irrespective of race or creed on December 23, 1876, or a few months after his accession to the throne, was the logical sequence of the Hatti-Humayoun. But the first promulgation of the Turkish constitution, Great Britain's failure to support its advocates and the exile of their great leader, Midhat Pasha, the prorogation of the short-lived first Turkish parliament and the recall of the constitution, and the steadily gained ascendency of Russian influence in Ottoman politics since the Russo-Turkish War of 1877–78, and in spite of the checks of the Treaty of Berlin, are all matters of a time subsequent to that which at present interests us.

CHAPTER IV

THE ROMANIST EMANCIPATION

The dealings of the Armenian church with the papacy date back to the end of the twelfth and the beginning of the thirteenth century. Taking advantage of the friendly relations of the Crusaders with the Armenian princes of Cilicia and joining with the emperor Henry VI in conferring upon Prince Leo II of that land a crown and the title of king (1198), Pope Celestine III established a sort of protectorate over Cilicia which his successors were long to exploit in the interest of their spiritual designs. This was the easier as the Armenian catholicate had been in 1147 removed to Romkla on the Euphrates on the eastern borders of Cilicia, and in 1294 was transferred to Sis, the capital of the kingdom.

This is not the place to go into the details of a long conflict between the Romanizing policy of the Armenian court on the one hand, and the nationalism of the nobility and populace on the other. It consists of resolutions of church councils, of repeated attempts to alter the ritual of the national church, of popular tumult and fanaticism, of murders and executions. There is nothing in history to match it, unless it be the last days of the Byzantine empire, when the disheartened emperors and their bishops negotiated peace with Rome at the cost of strife at home. As to the net results of that conflict, suffice it to say that it accomplished little more than to hasten the downfall of the Cilician kingdom, and only served to prove that Armenian nationalism and bigotry were more than a match for papal diplomacy and intrigue.[1]

An active propaganda of Romanist teaching, however, met with better success than these. The first papal missionary to the Armenians was the Dominican Bartholomew of Bologna, pupil of Thomas Aquinas, in the first instance sent out by Pope John XXII to Persia. Upon the invitation of an Armenian admirer, Bartholomew came from Maragha in Persia to Kerni near Nakhichevan, called a conference of friendly Armenian ecclesiastics, and with the object of disseminating the doctrines of Rome among the Armenians organized the Dominican order of the United Brethren. This was about the year 1330. Bartholomew was consecrated by the Pope archbishop of Greater Armenia, and for three hundred years his successors resided at Abaran near

[1] The union effected between the eastern and western churches at the council of Florence (1439), which met sixty-four years after the fall of the kingdom of Cilicia, was not indorsed by the Armenian people any more than by the Greek who preferred the turban of the Sultan to the tiara of the Pope. Barely had the legates of the catholicos to that council subscribed their names to the Chalcedonian teaching of "two natures," and to the Latin doctrines of the double procession of the Spirit, of purgatory, and of the supremacy of the Pope, when a national synod of the Armenians pronounced the patriarchal chair transferred to Etschmiadzin, and the catholicos of Cilicia sank into the position of a provincial primate (1441). Chamchean, *Armenian History*, Vol. III, pp. 473–92.

Nakhichevan. Here centered the activities of the Brethren who went on missionary tours in all directions. The work made such headway that early in the sixteenth century, according to a report submitted to Pope Clement VII (1523–34), the total number of papal Armenians aggregated 14,430, and the total number of the Brethren was 180. The Brethren represented the extreme Romanizing element among the Armenian people. They denied the validity of the orders and baptism of the Armenian church, and insisted on the rigid conformity of the Armenians to the Church of Rome in doctrine and worship. The order naturally became an element of great disturbance.

Subsequent to the Reformation in Europe, and the founding of the Propaganda at Rome (1622), the Latin missions among the Armenians, which had been for some time declining, received a new impetus. Clement Galanus, a Theatin monk, came to work among the Armenians of Constantinople in 1641. The Jesuits in 1650 established themselves at New Julfah, and in 1688 founded a mission at Erzroom, which was soon divided into two branches—the one, known as the Mission of St. Gregory the Illuminator, extending its operations to Hassan-Khaleh, Kars, and Bayezid, with their suburbs to the east of that city; the other, known as the Mission of St. Ignatius Loyola, extending its operations over Baiboort, Trebizond, Gumush-Haneh, and the surrounding country to the west. Under the powerful protection of the French

government the Latin missions again prospered.
Toward the end of the seventeenth century the dis-
sensions between papists and Gregorians at the
Turkish capital came to a head, and during the opening years of the following century, mainly under the
patriarch Avedick, occurred the first great persecution of the papal Armenians of Turkey. In 1707,
when persecution was renewed, the papal Armenians
of Constantinople ceased to attend the national
churches, and began to frequent the churches of the
Franks and to celebrate mass in private homes.
Seven years later (1714) they first conceived the idea
of constituting themselves an independent civil community. Steadily, also, Catholicism gained ground in
the cities of Asia Minor and Armenia. By 1735 the
Catholics of Angora had become powerful enough to
be able to seize four of the seven Armenian churches
of that city. In 1742 the Pope established the
Armenian patriarchate of the Lebanon with jurisdiction over Syria and Cilicia, and in 1758 appointed
an Armenian pontifical vicar at Constantinople,
with jurisdiction over Constantinople, Armenia, and
Asia Minor outside of Cilicia, and with authority
to ordain priests, subject to the approval of the Latin
pontifical vicar at the capital.

The eighteenth century was one of sore and repeated persecution for the papal Armenians. This
meant not only denial of the ordinances of the church,
but stripes, fines, tortures, exile, imprisonment, often
at hard labor, and even death. But early in the

last century more enlightened counsels prevailed for a while, and the authorities of the Armenian church made several efforts to draw rather than drive the Romanists back into the fold of the mother church. These efforts, however, no less than the persecutions which had preceded them, proved abortive. In 1810, in 1817, and again in 1820, efforts were made looking toward a reconciliation. The first effort failed because of opposition from the orthodox populace; the second, for lack of any response from the papal Armenian clergy; while the third was undertaken under government pressure, and was defeated by the resistance of a strong element from both parties.

The year 1820 marks an epoch in the history of Armenian Romanism in that it demonstrated conclusively to thoughtful minds the utter impossibility of reconciling Romanism and Armenian orthodoxy, and hence the necessity of according government recognition to the Romanists of Turkey as a separate sect. The year 1820 may be said to have commenced the process of the civil emancipation of the papal Armenians of the Turkish empire.

The interference of the Ottoman Porte in that year with the internal affairs of the Armenian church came about in this way. Through an intrigue of Halet Effendi, the Sultan's privy counselor, who owed them fabulous sums borrowed during the days of his embassy to the court of France (1813–15), the three Duzian brothers, managers of the imperial mint, were disgraced and cast into prison on a charge of embezzlement. As the Duzians, who were papal Armenians, failed to give surety from among the magnates of the Armenian community, their real and personal properties, together with those of all their connections, were declared forfeited to the government, and their residences were searched and despoiled. In the process of searching the residences of the Duzian tribe, the officers of government discovered in them rooms fitted up with altars for the celebration of mass. This proof of religious nonconformity was eagerly seized upon by Halet. On the strength of it the death-warrant of the Duzians was the more speedily secured, and on October 16, 1819, one of them, with a cousin, was hanged at the window of his own residence at Yenikeuy on the Bosphorus, while the other two were beheaded at the gate of the imperial palace, hard by the mint, where their severed heads were exposed to public view, with superscriptions attached stating their double offence, namely, having embezzled 120,000,-000 piastres (at that time equivalent, perhaps, to $17,000,000) from the treasury of the mint, and having converted their home into a place of worship. Many of the Duzian tribe, both men and women, also, were at this time sent into exile in distant islands and provinces of the empire. Thus awakened once again to the religious dissensions which rent the Armenian community, the Porte, on January 30, 1820, sent strict orders to the Armenian patriarchate to heal the existing breach and to suppress the illegal worship which was being maintained in papal homes.

Already the fall of the Duzians had become the signal for another persecution of papal Armenians. On January 25, 1820, the patriarch Paul banished the Armenian pontifical vicar and several of his clergy from the capital. Meantime he called up one by one the magnates and artisans of the Romanist party and asked them to sign the following declaration of loyalty: "Whatsoever the holy orthodox Armenian church accepts from the day of our holy Gregory the Illuminator until the present time, I accept, and whatsoever it rejects, I reject." On January 26, seeing that many in spite of threats refused to sign such an unqualified declaration, there was substituted for it the Nicene Creed which all Romanists signed without hesitation.

But upon receipt of instructions from the Porte to pacify the community and to suppress all heresy, Balian, the imperial architect, and Bezjian, who had succeeded the Duzian brothers as manager of the imperial mint, with other orthodox magnates, took the matter in hand and endeavored to bring about a peaceable solution of the community's ecclesiastical difficulties. These magnates recommended to the patriarch Paul the most conciliatory measures at his command, and promised their hearty support to every effort looking toward an amicable settlement of the community's troubles.

The papal Armenian clergy were at this time

divided into two main factions. On the one hand was the party of the Collegians, which derived its name from the leading one of a number of religious orders of which it was composed. The order of the Collegians had its headquarters at Rome, and was named after the College of the Propaganda in that city where its candidates for the priesthood received their training. To the party of the Collegians belonged the Armenian pontifical vicar of Constantinople, and the party had a large following especially among the papal Armenians of Angora in Asia Minor who constituted the largest and most bigoted papal community in the provinces. This party looked askance at everything that savored of a concession to Armenian orthodoxy.

On the other hand was the party of the Mekhitarists, whose headquarters was the convent of St. Lazarus at Venice. Of these there were about twenty at this time at Constantinople, having an important following among the people, including the great Duzian family and their connections. This party was distinguished by a more faithful adherence to the traditions of the national church than the other allowed, and a lesser emphasis on the supremacy of the bishop of Rome. The friends of unity in the mother church found their support in this party.

Father Mesrop was known as the leader of the Mekhitarists at Constantinople. This ecclesiastic was interviewed by the three Armenian magnates,

Balian, Bezjian, and Aznavourian, who proposed
to him a conference between the papal Armenian
clergy on the one hand and the learned men of the
national church on the other on the points of difference and the possible grounds of reconciliation between Romanists and Gregorians. "And, pray,"
said they, "let us not for the traditions of men and
for usages of late adoption make void God's covenant of love. But should your clergy be unwilling
to give their assent to this, let them know that they
will thereby throw open for their people the flood-
gates of penalty and persecution; for, behold, the
patriarch is under orders to report to the government
those who are intractable." The proposal of the
Armenian magnates met with a ready response from
Father Mesrop, who sent a messenger to communi-
cate the words of the Armenian magnates to the
papal Armenians, and to invite their clergy (some of
whom had been in hiding in the churches of the
foreign Catholics since the fall of the Duzians) to a
conference with the learned men of the national
church.

Thus two committees of three each were appointed
by the patriarch and by the Mekhitarists respectively.
During the months of February and March these
committees met in conference alternately at the
homes of the magnates Balian and Bezjian. The
subjects of their discussions were the five points over
which papists and orthodox Armenians had wrangled
for centuries, namely, (1) the Catholic Christology,

(2) the double procession of the Spirit, (3) the doctrine of purgatory, (4) the supremacy of the Pope, and (5) the sacrament of extreme unction. As a result of these deliberations a declaration of faith was drawn up which, after being referred to the patriarch, was to be laid before and adopted in the name of the nation by a general synod of bishops and priests and representatives of the trades. This document, which avowedly embodied the old orthodoxy of the Armenian church, pronounced on the five points above mentioned substantially as follows:

1. Christ is both truly God and truly man. The Armenian church maintains the doctrine of one nature as against the heresy of Nestorius, in which case the term is equivalent to "one personality." It holds to the docrine of two natures, however, in opposition to the heresy of Eutyches.

2. The Holy Spirit is the Spirit both of the Father and of the Son, *proceeding* from the Father and *taking* from the Son (cf. John 16:14). "The Father is self-subsistent, the Son is of the Father, the Holy Spirit is of them and in them."—*Teaching of Gregory the Illuminator*.

3. For those who die in the guilt of only venial sins, and for those who die in mortal sins forgiven but unatoned, prayers are offered by the church, mass is said, and alms are given. The abode of the souls of the repentant dead who thus need the good offices of the church is called by the Armenians a

sojourn, while by the Latins it is more specifically described as *purgatory.*

4. Peter is the head of the apostles and the Rock upon which all churches are founded, and as the apostles were vested by Christ with apostolic authority, so their lawful successors also are vested with all apostolic authority according to their several ranks.

5. The sacraments of the church are seven in number, one of them being extreme unction, which should be administered to those who are dangerously ill by the anointing with olive-oil consecrated by a priest.

All these declarations were more or less in the nature of a compromise between Latin and Armenian orthodoxy. The Armenians retained their doctrine of "one nature" while conceding the substance of the Romanist contentions on the person of Christ; they recognized a general sort of double relation to the Father and the Son in the Spirit without explicitly affirming the double procession of the Spirit; the prayers for the dead offered by the Armenian church were declared to be practically an admission of the doctrine of purgatory, but the name was not adopted; the gradation of apostolic authority in the church was acknowledged, but the ecclesiastical supremacy of the bishop of Rome was left a matter of inference only; and the anointing with olive-oil was declared, contrary to Armenian usage, a necessary adjunct of extreme unction, while the consecration of the oil was, contrary to papal usage, made the function of parish priests rather than of bishops.

On April 18, 1820, Paul summoned a general synod at the patriarchal church. There were present on the occasion the bishops and priests, and the magnates and clerks of guilds of Constantinople, besides the catholicos of Sis, and the legates of the sees of Etschmiadzin and Jerusalem. At this synod the declaration of faith agreed upon by the mixed committee was adopted, along with supplementary articles promising (in compliance with an imperial edict secured by Father Mesrop through his personal friend, Halet Effendi) to expurgate the anathema against Pope Leo the Great and the Council of Chalcedon from the Hymnal and the Ordinal of the church, to accept all councils and patristic writings which harmonized with the first three ecumenical councils, and to drop the names of John of Worodn and Gregory and Moses of Datev (fourteenth-century anti-Catholic writers canonized in the last quarter of the eighteenth century) from the ceremonial of the mass. Thus the negotiations for reunion were brought to an apparently successful issue, and a beginning was made of an actual reunion when seven of the ten papal clerics who had taken an active part in the negotiations, Father Mesrop being one of them, entered (not indeed without hesitation and not until constrained by government orders) the communion of the national church (April 30, 1820).

But this union received scant sympathy from any except those who directly participated in it. The Collegians who led by far the greater portion of the seven thousand papal families of the capital did all in their power from the beginning to frustrate the Mekhitarists' efforts toward reunion. They secured the influence of the French ambassador to induce the Latin pontifical vicar at Constantinople to recall a former decision allowing the papal Armenian clergy to participate in the proposed doctrinal discussions with the "schismatic" Armenians, and when the union had been actually consummated they persuaded that prelate to issue a bull of excision and anathema against the papal Armenian clergy who had been instrumental in effecting it. The hesitancy of the Mekhitarists about going into the Armenian church was not without justification.

Nor was the Armenian populace a whit better pleased. It was generally maintained that the patriarch of Constantinople, whose ecclesiastical powers were in no wise greater than those of a common diocesan bishop, had no right to convene a council to pass on doctrinal matters of interest to the church at large. On July 24 the Patriarch Paul further incensed the populace by consecrating olive-oil for use in the administration of extreme unction and distributing it among the churches of the city. There was needed only the touch of a spark to set the whole community in a blaze.

And that spark was soon forthcoming. On

August 19 a crafty Angora papist, taking in his hand a copy of the *Call to Love*—a pamphlet published in the preceding May embodying the plan of union as adopted by the synod—in which he had replaced the picture of the Illuminator with a portrait of the Pope, went to the quarter of the Armenian shoe-makers—a bigoted set of Cesareans among whom a fire of fanaticism could easily be kindled—and as he went the rounds of the shops, he said: "Why do you sit here idle, brethren? Do you not know that our patriarch has renounced our holy father the Illuminator and has received in his stead the Pope of the Franks? Look at this portrait! Does this look like our own Illuminator? The patriarch has despised the seat of Etschmiadzin, and has sworn allegiance to the chair of Rome. No more for our children the holy *muron* with which they may be sealed in the Holy Spirit, but olive-oil fit only for salads! Arise, brethren, arise, and join the three hundred that go tomorrow in a body to the patriar-chate to protest against such apostasy." Word went around from the heads of the shoemakers' guild that anyone failing to appear the next day at the patri-archate would be expelled from the trade. The patriarch was advised of the commotion the same evening and sent word about it to Balian and Bezjian, but too late in the night for them to be able to take any measures to avert the coming storm. On Sunday morning, the 20th, the zealous partisan of the Colle-gians was still engaged in his work of agitation. The

commotion spread in all directions like wild fire.
From all quarters of the city the men poured in, until
there was an immense mob surrounding the patriarchal church and vociferously demanding an explanation from the community's head. The patriarch
sent out two of his bishops to assure the men that he
had not turned Frank; but they were beaten and
driven away. This done the mob proceeded to the
patriarchate, close by, broke in the doors, and went
through the building in search of the patriarch.
Fortunately for all concerned, Paul had escaped by
a rear window and taken refuge in a neighboring
Moslem house. The riot was only quelled by the
agha of the Janissaries who came to the scene of
the trouble with five or six hundred troops, arrested
some, dispersed the rest, and left a guard to protect
the patriarchate.

The community paid dearly for this demonstration.
The grand vizier, failing to discover the ringleaders
through the Armenian patriarchate, took the matter
in his own hands.   On the day following the demonstration some members of the shoemakers' guild had
gone to the Porte and submitted a written protest
against the action of the patriarch in the cause of
union. The grand vizier had had them all arrested
and imprisoned, saying, "You should have done this
in the first instance." These men were subjected
to torture, and the names of five persons were presently elicited, some of them partially guilty and
some wholly innocent of instigating the demonstra-

tion. These five were seized—the original agitator
was not to be found, as his friends had hurried him
abroad—and after all possible information, real or
imaginary, had been wrung from them under severe
tortures, were on September 30 executed in various
parts of the city—one of them, an old man of eighty
years of age, being beheaded at the door of the patriarchal church. A number of magnates also were
at this time condemned to exile as indirectly responsible for the demonstration, among them being
Aznavourian, Balian, and Bezjian.

When the community had been thus ruthlessly
pacified, the patriarch turned his attention to the
papal Armenian priests who had been received into
the church. Their presence at Constantinople was
an eyesore to the populace of both parties. He was
planning to send them to distant points: two to
Etschmiadzin, two to Moush, and three to Jerusalem. No sooner, however, were they advised of his
intentions than they fled to the foreign Catholic
churches at Pera, performed penance for their apostasy, and returned again to the bosom of the Church
of Rome. Those of their people who had followed
them into the Armenian church followed them back
into the Romanist fold (May, 1821). And thus
ended the efforts of 1820 for peace and unity in the
Armenian community.

It was now becoming apparent that the position of
the papal Armenians was an anomalous one. Without
recognition from the Turkish government they were

a proscribed sect to be forced into conformity with the mother church; yet there was no power, ecclesiastical or civil, that could restore them to the mother church, or make them welcome there once they were restored.   Here was a problem.   And there seemed to be only one solution for it possible.   The papists must be accorded civil recognition of some sort. And one man at least there was who saw that solution.   That was Haroutioun Bezjian.

Bezjian (1771–1834) was one of the remarkable characters of Mahmoud's reign.   The son of an emigrant from Kars, he was born to poverty and obscurity, and had received but a rudimentary education in the patriarchal academy when at the age of twelve years he entered the employ of a silk-dealer as errand-boy.   Yet by dint of personal worth and native talent and with the help of the Duzians whom he first served and later (1819) succeeded in the imperial mint, he climbed up in the social and civic scale until he attained to the highest place ever given by an Ottoman ruler to one of Christian birth.

Sultan Mahmoud esteemed him as one of his wisest counselors.   In 1829, during the war with Russia, when famine threatened the Sultan's capital, it was Bezjian's counsel that led Mahmoud to remit all import duties on grain and provisions and thus to make a time of plenty possible once more.   After this war, too, Bezjian advised the depreciating of the currency, and thus made the payment of the first instalment of the indemnity of the war possible.

Sultan Mahmoud was so well pleased with this shortsighted but temporarily effective bit of financiering, that he conferred upon Bezjian the Decoration of the Imperial Image, raised him to the rank of a prince of the imperial court, and gave him the privilege of sharing in the deliberations of the imperial divan. From this time forward Bezjian was practically the most influential subject of the great Mahmoud. That his influence as adviser of the Sultan was not confined to civil and fiscal matters alone is evident from the fact that when the empire was in imminent peril from the invasion of Ibrahim Pasha (1833), it was Bezjian's advice that saved the day by inducing Mahmoud to seek the aid of Russia.

Bezjian used his influence at the palace on the whole for good. Intrigue was the very soul of Ottoman court life, and he did not wholly escape the spirit of his surroundings. But he was rather a shrewd man of the world than a sharp palace sycophant, and it certainly speaks well of his integrity and circumspection that at a time when no wealthy or influential man's life was safe, he lived to die a natural death.

In his own community Bezjian was held in very high esteem. He presided over the patriarch's advisory board, and thus wielded great power in the affairs of the Armenian community; but more than that, he was a friend of the poor, and of all educational, philanthropic, and religious enterprises, and constantly gave of his ample means for all sorts of benevolence. Powerful and well-beloved both in court and community, Bezjian of all men was the one most likely to make himself heard on the subject of the papal problem.

In 1820 Bezjian, recently appointed director of the mint, was already a man of considerable influence, and he took a prominent part in that year in the efforts for reunion in the Armenian church. Nor was he discouraged when he saw his efforts frustrated and ended in his own exile. Restored to favor at the end of a year, he turned his thoughts again to the papal problem, and when occasion presented itself he sought to apply to it the remedy which his failure had suggested to him. At his instance the Turkish government permitted the appointment of a papal Armenian priest, Anthony Nourijan, as civil agent for the papal Armenians, subordinate to the Armenian patriarchate (1827). Thus the papists received their first official recognition as a distinct civil-ecclesiastical body.

Bezjian's half-measure, however, encouraged the papists to aspire more fondly than ever to an independent patriarchate of their own. Nor was this surprising. Only it was unfortunate that their influential men should resort to the old tricks of court-intrigue—something which with Bezjian at the palace was but "kicking against the goad"—and thus bring upon themselves and their coreligionists the dread wrath of the Sultan.

For in the fall of 1827 the Tengerian brothers, Jacob and Joseph, represented to the Sultan that the eastern Armenians, who in the Russo-Persian war then in progress[1] were fighting shoulder to shoulder with the Russians, were planning soon to engage in hostilities against the Sultan's own dominions, and with the help of Russia to set up a kingdom of their own, and begged him, by constituting them into a separate community, to spare the papists the penalties which, if identified with the Armenian civil community, they might unjustly be made to share with the orthodox Armenians. How disquieting such words would prove to the Sultan will be realized when it is recalled that the Greek War of Independence was at this time still in progress.

The Sultan upon receiving the Tengerians' petition forthwith sent for Bezjian and laid it before him. Bezjian, after explaining to the Sultan the motives which he thought had prompted such libel, told him that the easiest way to dispel his fears was to send for the patriarch and demand that he should be security for the good conduct of his people. Garabed, the reigning patriarch, and the former patriarch Paul, were accordingly summoned to the Porte. And they took advantage of the occasion to balance accounts with the Romanists to the best

---

[1] This was the war of 1826–28 as a result of which that portion of Armenia lying between the Araxes and the Koor, with Etschmiadzin, the seat of the catholicos of the Armenian church, passed under Russian sovereignty.

of their ability. They declared to the grand vizier
that on the strength of the confessional they could
venture to go security for the good conduct of their
people in all parts of the Sultan's dominions, but that
for the papal Armenians who never came to confess
to Armenian priests, they could assume no responsibility.

The scheme of the Tengerians proved a boomerang.
On October 15, 1827, the government sent the Tengerian brothers and their families into exile. This
was the signal for another persecution. The battle
of Navarino which occured five days later, and the
consequent rupture with the European powers,
released the Sultan from all considerations of policy
in his treatment of the papal Armenians whom he
regarded as their sympathizers. By an edict of
January 11, 1828, he ordered the Armenian patriarch
to banish all papal Armenians from Angora residing
at the capital to their native town, and all other papal
Armenians who refused to submit to the patriarch's
civil and ecclesiastical jurisdiction to various points
in the interior. All Catholics not banished from
the capital were to be removed from the foreign
suburbs of the city where they resided, to Stamboul,
Scutari, and other Armenian quarters. The papal
Armenian clergy were to be banished to foreign parts.
Within two months the provisions of this decree had
been carried out to the letter. In the latter part of
January several thousand Angora papists were
banished to their native city, suffering untold hard-

ships on the way from cold and privation. Early in February all native papal Armenians were removed from the foreign suburbs of the city to Stamboul and Scutari, many of them being compelled to live in tents while their residences were sold to Turks at nominal prices. Later all Catholic Armenian priests that could be laid hands upon were banished from the empire, while early in March all nuns were exiled to interior villages. Meanwhile many papal Armenians, both of the capital and of the provinces, who refused to return to the communion of the church were exiled to different points in Asia Minor, while some fled to Russia, to the Island of Syra, and to Trieste, suffering much destitution in the lands of their willing exile. The number of the exiles aggregated 12,000. It is estimated that of hardships incident to this persecution four hundred children perished.

But this was to be the last tribulation for the papal Armenians. At the close of the Russo-Turkish War of 1828–29 the two Roman-Catholic powers, France and Austria, united in demanding of the Sultan the recall of the exiles and the establishment of an independent civil organization for the papists of Turkey. Early in January, 1830, the exiles were accordingly permitted to return to their homes, their properties were restored to them, and papal Armenians generally were allowed all freedom of worship on the simple condition that they should have their own churches and not frequent the churches of the foreign Catholics in the country. In the following year the papists were accorded formal civil recognition.

At first the papists of Turkey had two heads at Constantinople, the one civil and the other ecclesiastical. Anthony Nourijan, appointed civil agent for the papists in 1827, was consecrated by the Pope archbishop, with jurisdiction over the native papists of Constantinople, Armenia, and Asia Minor outside of Cilicia, while Jacob Manuelian was elected civil head of the papal community throughout the empire, and confirmed by imperial edict under the title of "Bishop of the Catholics." But under Anthony Hasounian, whose accession occurred in 1846, the two offices of archbishop and civil head were combined in one person. In the year 1866 the spiritual powers of the papal patriarch[1] at Constantinople were made to extend, like his civil powers, over the whole empire, by Hasounian's election to succeed Peter VIII as patriarch of the Lebanon.

The imperial edict which established the papal civil community in the Turkish empire, and defined its privileges, was issued on January 5, 1831, and runs as follows:

WHEREAS the Catholic rayahs of the Ever-abiding Government and Eternal Empire of the Ottomans have hitherto, being without a bishop of their own, been under the jurisdiction of the Greek and Armenian patriarchs, and thus, on

[1] The Turkish government permitted the recognized head of the papal community to call himself "Patriarch" in 1835.

account of the Catholic rites being different from the Greek
and Armenian, have been unable to observe their own rites,
and, compelled to attend the churches of the Franks and to
ask non-Catholics to perform their marriage ceremonies for
them, have endured distress and inconvenience, as I have
ascertained and know; and

WHEREAS since early days they have been subjects of the
Ottoman empire enjoying the imperial protection,

Therefore, I, on this 21st day of the holy month of Rejeb,
in the year of the Hegira 1246, in order that they may henceforth refrain from attending the churches of the Franks and
be able to observe their rites in their own proper churches,
and thus being relieved from the distress and hardships of
former times, enjoy peace and quiet (a due regard to which
is expected from a ruler who loves his subjects), have appointed
by this August Mandate, bishop over all the Catholics—both
those living in my Imperial City, and those living in other
parts of my dominions—and have designated, by the August
Imperial Seal, as the representative of the Catholic Christian
community, a subject by birth, approved and elected by them,
namely, the Vartabed Jacob Manuelian (may his latter end
be happy!), granting this August Imperial Rescript on the
condition that he pay the donative of 150,000 akjes in advance into my Imperial Treasury, and, further, year by year
pay into the Income Treasury 3,038,000 akjes[1] as an annual
tribute. Thus I have ordained that henceforth the Vartabed
Jacob be recognized as bishop by both great and small among
the Catholics, and that they do not depart from his word in
the matter of their rites, or allow others to interfere with the
same.

And in case the bishop of the Catholics shall, pursuant to
their regulations, effect changes in the appointment of the
provincial vartabeds, no one shall interfere. Neither shall

---

[1] These sums were equivalent at this time to about $81 and
$1,645 respectively, but much more in purchasing power.

any changes be effected in the personnel of the provincial vartabeds without the initiative of the said bishop.

And vartabeds of other communities shall not solemnize
any mixed marriages to which members of this community
shall be parties contrary to its regulations or without its
bishop's knowledge and sanction.

If the wife of a rayah of this community desert him, or a
rayah divorce or marry a wife, no one but the agents of the
bishop shall intervene or interfere.

All matters of marriage and divorce, and, the consent being
mutual, causes between two rayahs, in this community, shall
be under the jurisdiction of the bishop; and the officers of
government shall not interfere with his legal decisions or with
his administering oaths in the church according to the community's regulations.

The bishop shall confiscate for the annual tribute all
properties of Catholic vartabeds and nuns of the community
dying heirless, and officers of the department of the Imperial
Treasury or of the Bureau of Legacies, or other officers of
government, shall not interfere. Wills made by the Catholic
vartabeds or nuns, or others of the Catholic rayahs, according
to custom, in favor of the church's poor or of the bishop,
shall be valid, and shall be duly probated.

Wherever the vartabeds appointed by the bishop for the
purpose of collecting incomes from church property and gifts
for the support of the clergy shall go, they shall not be
molested.

And none shall interfere with the bishop's scepter, or the
horse that he rides, or his men, their uniforms and properties,
or the conveyance to the bishop's residence of the products
regularly allowed him for his support, such as sweet cider,
honey, oil, and the like.

And of the ten men doing errands for, and engaged in the
general service of, the bishop, no capitation tax, dues, or
imposts shall be demanded.

Trials of members of this community for sedition shall be held nowhere other than in the Court of Appeals.

All vineyards and orchards and other real estate willed to the poor of the church, as well as all church property, shall be under the jurisdiction of the bishop, and none shall interfere therewith.

Should there be any vartabeds of this community who, without the bishop's permission, go from place to place and raise disturbance, the bishop shall restrain them.

Neither the Greek and Armenian patriarchs with their constituency, nor anyone else, shall in any manner interfere with its affairs.

Let all concerned know my will, and respect my signature.

Given in the year of the Hegira 1246, in the month of Rejeb, the 21st.[1]

That Romanism ever gained a foothold among the Armenians is no cause for surprise. Its clean-cut theology, the absoluteness and exclusiveness of its claims, the superiority of its clergy to the native Armenian in point of education and discipline, and in general its cultivation of the new enlightenment through foreign intercourse, all combined from the first to render Armenian Romanism a movement of undeniable power.

During the three-fourths of a century which have elapsed since the emancipation, the number of papal Armenians in the Turkish empire has perhaps doubled. It is at present estimated at about 86,000.[2]

[1] Berberian, *Armenian History*, pp. 217 ff.

[2] Distributed among the various dioceses as follows: Constantinople, 16,000; Adana, 1,500; Aleppo, 7,500; Diarbekir, 5,000; Angora, 8,000; Brousa, 3,000; Cesarea, 1,500; Erzroom, 10,000; Harpoot, 1,700; Marash, 6,000; Merdin, 8,000; Malatia, 4,000;

That the growth has not been greater is to be accounted for by a variety of reasons. In the first place, the denationalizing policy of Rome, and the arrogant claims of the papacy, have proved a serious obstacle to the progress of Romanism among the Armenians. Further, with the gradual reformation of the Armenian clergy in education and discipline, the causes for disaffection on the part of the people with the mother church have slowly disappeared. Again, with the progress of enlightenment, it has been more and more clearly perceived by the Armenian laity how trifling is the practical difference between the papal and the Armenian church—the progress of lay education, and the broader outlook upon life which it has involved, have caused the old dogmatic and controversial differences to lose their force. And as the last, but by no means least, of the reasons for the slow growth of Armenian Romanism since the emancipation, may be mentioned the rise of Armenian Protestantism, which has not only made common cause with the orthodox Armenians against the Roman propaganda, but has also, while meeting the real needs which Romanism had met, offered, in addition, something which Romanism knew not how to bestow.

Moush, 6,000; Sivas and Tocat, 3,000; Trebizond, 5,000. Cf. *Missiones Catholicae Cura S. Congregationis de Propaganda Fide Descriptae Anno 1895.* The total number of papal Armenians throughout the world approximates 140,000.

CHAPTER V

PAULICIANISM AGAIN

Paulicianism first makes its appearance in history under that name in the seventh century, when the Paulician leader, Constantine, from the Armenian district of Mananali, southeast of the modern Erzroom,[1] brought the sect under the notice of the western world by carrying its doctrines into Pontus and Cappadocia. In the apparent partiality of Constantine and his followers for the Apostle Paul, of which the custom of naming the Paulician leaders and congregations respectively after the associates and churches of the apostle to the gentiles was cited as an instance, modern scholars, beginning with Gibbon, thought they found the explanation of the name Paulician. This, however, was a mistaken opinion. For, as Professor Conybeare has lately pointed out, the Paulicians are to be identified with the *Pauliani* of an earlier age who derived their name not from Paul the apostle but from Paul of Samosata.[2]

For a period of one hundred and fifty years from the time of Constantine the history of the Paulicians

---

[1] Not near Samosata, as Photius has led so many modern writers to believe. See Chamchean, *Armenian History*, Vol. II, p. 886, and Conybeare, *Introduction to "The Key of Truth,"* p. lxix.

[2] Conybeare, *ibid.*, pp. cv ff.

is one of constant persecution at the hands of the orthodox emperors of Byzantium. Justinian II in the seventh century, and Michael I and Leo V, in the ninth, when not incited by bigotry, persecuted these heretics with the hope of redeeming their own reputation for orthodoxy. But the empress Theodora, the restorer of the images of the orthodox church, surpassed them all in persecuting zeal, and the Greek chroniclers have recorded with pride that during her regency no less than 100,000 Paulicians were destroyed by hanging, crucifixion, decapitation, and drowning.

In the ninth century the Paulicians, in alliance with the Saracens, for once wreaked fierce vengeance upon their Byzantine persecutors. Emerging from their fortified town of Tephrike, the modern Divrik, they overthrew the armies of the empire, and overran Asia Minor as far as Nicomedia and Ephesus. At this time the Paulicians destroyed many images and relics of the Greek saints, and turned the cathedral of Ephesus into a horse stable. This, however, was only a temporary outburst of Paulician power and exasperation. With the fall of their great leader Chrysocheir the military glory of the Paulicians passed away, and as before, so after that event, they remained a sect sorely oppressed and persecuted.

Emperors who sympathized with their cause sometimes pursued a middle course. A race of warlike mountaineers, the Armenian Paulicians, so dangerous to the empire, when in alliance with the Saracens, on its eastern borders, could be employed as the empire's trusted guardians on its western. So the Iconoclast, Constantine Copronymus, in the eighth century, and the Armenian, John Zimisces, in the tenth, transplanted these heretics by the thousands from the regions of Erzroom and Melitine to the borderlands of Thrace. There, while the Paulician soldier guarded the line of the Danube against the barbarians, the Paulician missionary laid the foundations of the Bogomile church of the Bulgarians and scattered in Europe the seeds of a reformation which bore its full fruitage in a later age.[1]

The Armenian church persecuted these heretics no less than the Greek, and the more violently the more Byzantine influence and power were felt east of the anti-Taurus mountains. The Armenian synod of Tevin (719) enjoined upon the faithful to shun and to hate these "children of the devil and kindlers of the eternal fire." And the Paulicians of Armenia were shunned and hated by their orthodox fellow-countrymen. Often they were hunted like wild beasts. They were scourged and imprisoned. They were branded on the forehead with the image of a fox (Song of Solomon 2:15). They were deprived of their eyesight. They were burned at the stake. They were driven wholesale out of their homes, and their villages were destroyed. It was

[1] A degenerate, Romanized remnant of the Paulicians of Europe survived to our own times. See Conybeare, *Introduction*, pp. cxxxviii f., and Hamlin, *Among the Turks*, pp. 265 ff.

no meaningless vow that the Armenian Paulician *elect one* took, to endure "scourgings, imprisonments, tortures, reproaches, crosses, blows, sufferings, and all the tribulations of the world."[1]

The last persecution of the Paulicians of the Middle Ages in Armenia of which a record has been preserved was conducted in the middle of the eleventh century by Gregory Magistros, duke of Vasbouragan and Daron (the modern provinces of Van and Moush respectively). At this time the town of Tonrak, near the modern Bayezid, was the great Paulician center in Armenia, and had been ever since the ninth century when the Paulician leader, Smpad of Zarehaven, made it his headquarters. Gregory Magistros destroyed Tonrak and renamed it after St. George, and had over a thousand of the Tonrakians, as the Armenian Paulicians were now called, baptized and confirmed in the orthodox church.[2]

Until comparatively recent years it was the general impression in the West that since the time of Nerses the Graceful, of the twelfth century, who was the last Armenian writer to make mention of it, Armenian Paulicianism had become totally extinct. But the heresy which was exiled to the western borders of the Byzantine empire, only to live on to scatter the seeds of religious dissent in the western world, had also lingered on through the centuries to our

[1] *The Key of Truth* (Conybeare's Armenian text), p. 44.

[2] For a review of the history of the Paulicians of the Middle Ages in Armenia see Conybeare, *Introduction*, pp. lvii–lxxi.

own day in Armenia itself. The region lying between Erzroom and Moush was always a hotbed of
Armenian Paulicianism, and here, like Constantine
of Mananali in the seventh century, and Jacob of
Hark in the eleventh, rose the Paulician leader,
John Shoushdak-Vartabedian[1] in the eighteenth.
Vartabedian was persecuted at Moush as the representative of a detested sect, and fled, about 1775, to
Constantinople. From Constantinople he went to
the Mekhitarist convent at Venice; but his heretical
notions were there quickly detected, and he was
compelled a few days after arrival to return to
the Turkish capital. Here he was arrested and
sentenced to imprisonment at hard labor, and, to
escape further persecution, he made a profession of
Islam. Shortly afterward he returned to Armenia,
and, after extorting ordination with the backing
of the Turkish kadi of Khnus from a bishop then
residing in the vicinity of Manazkert, commenced
an active propaganda of his heresy in Maroukh,
Khnus, Tschevirmé, and other villages of the Khnus
district. For this crime he was loaded with chains
and sent to Etschmiadzin, but he escaped from
prison and went back again to his field of labor "to
spread his poison." In the year 1801, his patron,
the kadi of Khnus, having been executed, he was
forced by the Turks to return to Islam. His subsequent history is not known; but it is clear that by

---

[1] The name is given in an article in the *Puragn* of Constantinople for August 13, 1892.

that date he had done very effective work in the region of Khnus.[1]

In February, 1837, Garabed, former bishop of the Erzroom diocese, directed the attention of the Synod of Etschmiadzin to Vartabedian's followers. Garabed was at the time bishop of the Armenians of Georgia, but he was well informed on the affairs of his former flock, as well those who at the close of the Russo-Turkish War of 1828–29 had emigrated under his leadership into the Tzar's newly acquired Armenian territories, as those who still remained in their old homes in Turkish Armenia.

Garabed wrote to the Synod that in the village of Arkhveli, in Russian Armenia, there were twenty-five households of Armenian immigrants from the village of Tschevirmé, in the diocese of Erzroom, who professed the heresy of the Tonrakians. Upon this the Synod dispatched to Arkhveli two priests to make an investigation. These priests called the people of the village together, and, after reading to them the bull of the Synod, made an effort to discover the heretics in their midst. As all the confession they were at first able to elicit was the orthodox one, "We are children of the Illuminator," they confronted the people with some from neighboring villages with whom they had had intercourse, and the people then reluctantly confessed that they had

[1] Basil Sargisian, *A Study of the Sect of the Manichaean-Paulician Tonrakians, and the Epistle of Gregory of Narek*, pp. 101 ff.

known a priest in Khnus who had taught the heresy
in question, but affirmed that they had not only
refused to receive him, but had "anathematized him
with anathemas," that the priest was now dead, and
that while it was true that some of them had talked
of his heresy in private conversation, it had been
only through ignorant foolishness on their part.
Finally, they gave a written promise "forever to
repudiate the evil heresy and to remain steadfast in
the confession and the laws of the orthodox Armenian church." One of the priests was afterward
commissioned to reside at Arkhveli for the purpose
of completely rooting out the heresy.

The Synod, while concluding to resign to the
tribunal of God the judgment of the deceased Khnus
priest who had taught this heresy, resolved to make
an effort to destroy as far as possible the fruits of
his propaganda. The then bishop of Erzroom was
directed to seek out any remnants of heresy that
might still be lingering in the district of Khnus. At
the same time a request was addressed to Baron
Rosen, military governor of the Caucasus, "to direct
the local civil authorities to watch the conduct and
operations of the Armenian inhabitants of Arkhveli
with an eye to the heresy which has appeared in their
midst." Baron Rosen made inquiries as to the
nature of the heresy in question, to which the Synod
answered: "The heresy of the Tonrakians consists
in this, that they reject the mediation of saints, con-
temn their images, deny the use of fasts, repudiate

the value of prayers, reject the immaculateness of the Holy Virgin Mother of God, and the sacrament of baptism, etc."

This correspondence between the Synod and Governor Rosen was still in progress when, in December, 1837, an advice came to the Synod from the spiritual authorities of Gumri (Alexandropol), through the consistory of Erivan, that a certain Garabed Megrditschian of that village, who had only in the preceding July adopted the heresy of the Tonrakians, had made an important confession during sickness, and had divulged the names of seven others in Gumri, who, some alone and some with their entire families, had received the heresy of the Tonrakians from George and Souvar of Arkhveli, and who had now also made confession and indicated their repentance. These eight men, four of whom could read and write, made written recantations, from which we gather the following points of Paulician controversial teaching:

1. Christ is not God, but the Son of God, who was born a man of the Virgin Mary, suffered and died on the cross, rose again from the dead, and now sits on the right hand of the Father, making intercession for us.

2. The moral law, as given to Moses in the Decalogue, should be obeyed, but no trust should be reposed in external rites and observances. Making the sign of the cross and genuflections are superfluous. Pilgrimages to Etschmiadzin and Jerusalem

and the keeping of fasts are of human invention and unnecessary. The worship of crosses and pictures of saints is idolatry. The sacrifice of the mass is a lie, and the elements used in it are not the body and blood of Christ, but ordinary bread and wine. The baptism and holy ointment of the orthodox churches are false and only the mark of the Beast on the forehead, and a mere handful of water is all that is necessary for the administration of Christian baptism.

3. A priest should not be called "Lord, Lord" (Der-der), but only a clergyman (literally, "a man of orders"); for God alone is Lord. Confession to a priest is of no profit for the forgiveness of sins— the penitent should confess his sins to God alone. Neither can saints intercede for us.

4. Armenians, Russians, Georgians, and all others except the German Evangelicals,[1] are false Christians and idolaters whose baptism is not valid. The traditions of the church fathers have no binding authority, and the canons of the church councils were inspired by the devil. For the time being, however, an outward conformity to the church's requirements should be maintained by the faithful, so that, if possible, all the people may in time be converted to their faith.

The confessions of Gumri excited the Synod to

[1] Millennialists from Würtemberg who came to the Caucasus in 1817. See *Researches of Smith and Dwight in Armenia*, Vol. I, pp. 264 ff.

renewed activity, and appeal was again made to the governor of the Caucasus. A civil inquest was then instituted by the military governor of Tiflis, General Praigon, into the heresy of Arkhveli, and in the spring of 1838 it was discovered that the heretics of Arkhveli and Gumri were as active as ever. The Tonrakians of the former village then numbered thirty-three households, and, to ward off suspicion, had built themselves an orthodox church. Three years later it was discovered that in 1837 the heretics of Arkhveli had "baptized each other" by night in a stable and in a private room. Their baptism had been administered in connection with the Lord's Supper, wherein the elements used had been a loaf of plain unleavened bread baked in an oven, and wine served in a common vessel placed on a common wooden table. Upon the bread they had pronounced the words: "Take, eat; this is the body of our Lord Jesus Christ;" upon the wine, the words: "This is the blood of our Lord Jesus Christ." The candidate for baptism had approached the table uncovered, when the ministering officer had poured upon his head a first handful of water, saying: "In the name of the Father;" then a second handful, saying: "And of the Son;" then a third, saying: "And of the Holy Spirit. Amen." Whereupon the candidate had helped himself to a morsel of the bread and a drink of the wine.

General Praigon referred the case of the heretics to the provincial court of Gumri. Before the end

of April, 1841, however, there was issued a general
imperial amnesty, and in the following September
the court of Gumri advised the Synod of Etschmiadzin that the heretics of Arkhveli and Gumri had
under that amnesty been released from trial and
punishment.

The Synod, not satisfied with this decision of the
court, appealed to the governor. It was in reply
informed, in March, 1843, that the governor had
found the decision of the court invalid, inasmuch as
heretics did not come under the general head of
criminals amnestied by the edict, and had ordered
the further prosecution of the trial. In June, 1845,
the upshot of the whole matter was thus communicated to the Synod: The civil and criminal court of
Tiflis, having examined into the whole case, had
declared that the four leaders of heresy at Arkhveli,
among them George Sargisian, who called himself
a deacon, and Souvar Hohannessian, and the four
at Gumri, were, under the criminal laws of 1842,
subject to be drafted into the army; but inasmuch
as they had organized their sect before the promulgation of the amnesty of 1841, the court, pursuant to
the first article of that amnesty, had decided only to
demand the costs of each heretic's trial, 49 roubles
and 50 kopeks (about $25), and to send these eight
and their followers to the spiritual authorities of the
Armenian church to be dealt with by them according
to their own laws, at the same time forbidding
George Sargisian of Arkhveli to call himself a dea-

con, as he had failed to produce his credentials, and the authorities of the Armenian church refused to recognize him.

The Synod replied that such penalty was altogether incommensurate with the heinousness of the heresy in question, and petitioned the governor "that the guilty ones might be punished to the full extent of their grave transgressions against God, according to the proper sense of the law, just like other criminals."[1]

With this protest the episode seems to have closed. Two years before, Nerses of Ashdarak had been elected catholicos of all the Armenians, and in May, 1846, he arrived at Etschmiadzin and assumed the duties of his office. Nerses was an enlightened man; and we may presume that during his eleven years' active pontificate the Synod was restrained by him in its orthodox zeal against the Paulicians.

These heretics, however, must have endured much petty persecution at the hands of their neighbors during those years. At any rate some of them returned to their old homes in the district of Khnus, and at such a time as to render very material aid to the Protestant movement in that region. About 1847 two families of them removed to the village of Khnus, "where," says the American missionary at Erzroom, writing in 1852, "they have been exert-

[1] For a fuller account of the inquisition of 1837–45 see an article by Alexander Eritzian entitled "Tonrakian Armenians of Our Day," in the *Portz* of Tiflis, October, 1880.

ing their influence in a quiet way, till the number of
families persuaded of the correctness of their faith
amounts to eight, embracing about sixty souls."[1]
So promising was the outlook in Khnus that as early
as 1853 it was recommended that that village be
made a regular outstation of the mission of the American Board at Erzroom. About this time also Souvar
Hohannessian appears to have returned from Arkhveli to his old home in Tschevirmé; and in 1854 this
village is reported as having among its forty households four, with about forty souls, who are openly
Protestant, while by the year 1860 the number of
Protestants in the village has doubled.

And who can tell how much Protestant missions
in Armenia have been feeding on Paulician soil?
Khnus and Tschevirmé, those ancient strongholds
of Armenian Paulicianism, were not the only places
where Paulicianism became a feeder to modern
Protestantism. Eritzian states that in 1880 of the
one hundred and thirty-seven Protestant households
of Valarshabad (Neapolis), in the vicinity of Etschmiadzin, nearly three-quarters were originally Tonrakian. The same writer further states that the
Tonrakians were numerous at that date in the provinces of Shirak, Galzwan, Pambak, New Bayezid,
Erivan, and Etschmiadzin, associating in some
places with Russian heretics like the Molokans, and
in others with Protestants. A careful investigation

[1] *Missionary Herald*, December, 1852, pp. 359 f. The missionary is ignorant of the identity of these people.

on the ground will doubtless reveal a very close connection between this ancient heresy and modern Protestantism in Armenia.

But we must turn to what was the most important discovery of the inquisition of 1837–45. Sergius Haroutiounian of Gumri in the first year of that inquisition confessed that he had learned the teachings above detailed in 1835 of George of Arkhveli, and that the latter had in his possession a heretical manuscript entitled the *Key of Truth* which contained all those teachings. This disclosure led to the seizure of the manuscript, which, in February, 1838, the consistory of Erivan transmitted to the Synod. It is now preserved in the archives of the Synod, at Etschmiadzin. It is a copy, written on octavo paper in minuscule, of an ancient original the older portions of which perhaps go as far back as the ninth century, and contains the baptismal service and the ordinal of the Armenian Paulician church, together with a catechism, and some controversial matter bearing on various practices of the orthodox churches, like infant baptism, image worship, Mariolatry, and adoration of saints. We will now proceed to examine the contents of this document.[1]

[1] The attention of scholars was first called to this document and its contents by Eritzian in the *Portz* of Tiflis for October, 1880, and the text of it was published, with an introduction and English translation, by Conybeare in 1898. The manuscript is mutilated. Three whole chapters, all but the title and the opening words of another, and important portions of five others—

The *Key of Truth* is one of the few relics of primitive Christian thought now extant. No peculiarity of it is more striking at first sight than its practical scripturalness. One fails to find in this book that type of doctrine which was the product of Greek speculation, and originated in the councils and the controversies of the orthodox church. The *Key's* idea of a Christian is characteristic—not a man who has the orthodox doctrine, but simply one who knows the Lord Jesus and keeps his commandments (p. 56).[1] This fact should be borne in mind especially in examining the *Key's* ideas of the deity and of the person of Christ.

thirty-six pages out of the one hundred and forty-nine composing the body of the manuscript—were destroyed before its surrender, and numerous heretical words were carefully erased. If one who has not himself seen this manuscript may venture an opinion with regard to it, I should say that this is probably a copy made early in the last century from one which was made "in the province of Daron" in the year 1782. The error in the dating at the beginning of the manuscript—namely, 1882, instead of 1782, which is given at the end—seems to betray a scribe of the nineteenth century. It is of interest to note that according to testimony given by Paulicians of Arkhveli in 1838, the copy of 1782 was made at Tschevirmé by John Shoushdak-Vartabedian. This John's name, however, nowhere appears in our copy of the *Key of Truth*. The name at the beginning of the fragmentary colophon, John Vahakouni, must not be confused with it. The latter is not the name of a copyist, but of one of a number of persons who, according to what follows, had requested the making of a copy in 1782. For a discussion of the age of the *Key*, see Conybeare, *Introduction*, pp. xxix ff.

[1] This and all subsequent references are to Conybeare's Armenian text.

The theology of the *Key* is Unitarian of the so-called Monarchian type.   Having this ancient relic of Armenian Paulicianism in our hands today, we can see that Gregory Magistros had a clear understanding of Paulician tenets when he referred the origin of the Paulicians to the bishop of Antioch and third-century Monarchian leader, saying: "Here, then, you see the Paulicians who got their poison from Paul of Samosata."   Paul of Samosata was the chief exponent of what is known as Dynamic Monarchianism, or the view that Christ was not a distinct person within the Godhead, but a mere man on whom the impersonal Logos rested and in whom it dwelt through his ministry.

The orthodox writers emphasize the deity of Christ, find in the infant Jesus, God incarnate, and even go so far as to declare Mary to be Mother of God and David to be father of God.   The *Key*, on the other hand, lays emphasis on the undisguised humanity of our Lord.   Christ—so the *Key* teaches—was conceived by the Holy Ghost, and born the New Adam free from original or actual sin.   Nevertheless he was only a man, creature and not creator, and lived as such for thirty years.   At the beginning of his public ministry he was led by the Spirit to seek baptism at the hand of John; and when he was baptized he saw the Spirit descend upon himself, and heard the voice: "This is my beloved Son." Then, and not until then, was he endowed with divine powers and prerogatives.   For then it was that he received his "authority," and the offices of "high priest," "king," and "chief shepherd." Then was he "chosen," and "glorified," and "strengthened." Then he became "the light of the world," "the way, the truth, and the life." Then he became "the gate of heaven," "the foundation of our faith," and "the savior of us sinners." Then he was "filled with the Godhead;" then he became "the loved one," and "the lamb without blemish." "Then he also put on the former robe of light which Adam lost in Paradise. Then he was called upon by the Spirit of God to commune with the heavenly Father. And then he was appointed king over things in heaven and on earth and under the earth" (pp. 5, 6). The ascended Christ still enjoys these attributes; and no prayers in the *Key* are more fervent or beautiful than those addressed to him.

The fact that Christ was baptized during maturity is cited by the *Key* as the reason for the practice of exclusive adult baptism. As Christ did not receive baptism until he was old enough to be intelligently led by the Spirit of God, so, the *Key* argues, the believer should not be given the seal of his discipleship until he has attained to a responsible age. Nothing is more emphatically denounced in the *Key* than infant baptism. A child is unconscious of sin and incapable of repentance or faith, and therefore not a fit subject for baptism. For the Gregorian custom of baptism on the eighth day after birth, the *Key* substitutes a plain ceremony of name-giving (Luke 2:21). In support of the contention that baptism is not valid without the exercise of personal faith, such scriptures are appealed to as the following: "He that believeth and is baptized shall be saved; but he that believeth not shall be condemned" (Mark 16:16); "But when they believed Philip preaching good tidings concerning the kingdom of God and the name of Jesus Christ, they were baptized, both men and women" (Acts 8:12). As a corollary of this teaching, it is provided that converts from the Latin, Greek, and Armenian churches shall be rebaptized.

The *Key* contemplates but one true baptism, the baptism of a new life in Christ (of "regeneration"), which as such is the second of the Christian sacraments. Professor Conybeare's statement, therefore, that in the *Key* Christian baptism is "expressly identified with the baptism of John, which was not by the Spirit and fire, but by water only,"[1] is misleading. Rather is John's baptism subordinated to and identified with Christ's and his apostles'. John's baptism is spoken of as "the baptism of our Lord Jesus Christ" (p. 2). John's baptism, not less than Christ's own, has for its final object the Lord Jesus Christ; it is only the prelude of that message: "Behold the Lamb of God that taketh away the sin of the world" (pp. 3, 5). John himself preaches and teaches, calls to repentance and faith, then washes away the filth of the body—all preliminary to the

[1] *Introduction*, p. cxlvi.

Lord's bestowing "spiritual salvation" as the Lamb
of God and our Intercessor (p. 3). If Johannine
baptism receives any attention in the *Key* at all, it
does so only as Christ himself stands in it as its central figure. As a call to repentance it is something
more than merely a call to a renunciation of sins—it
is a call to faith, to a knowledge of Christ, and to a
baptism of the Spirit of the heavenly Father (pp. 3,
4). The baptism by water, in that case, unless it is
to be devoid of all meaning, must immediately be
followed by the believer's induction into Christian
discipleship. In itself a mere washing of the body,
it must become the occasion of a surrender of one-
self to Christ and an anointing by the Holy Spirit.

This conception—not of two baptisms essentially
different, but of one baptism in Christ, of which
John's ceremonial baptism is only a prelude and
type—is imaged in the baptismal service of the *Key*
in an interesting ritual (p. 33), which Professor
Conybeare's translation fails to bring out. As the
catechumen kneels in the water, the elect one pours
some water on his head, "*reserving the thought, the
form, and the intention*" of baptism—that is, without
yet actually administering the sacrament either in
thought and intention, or in the threefold pouring
of water—and merely as a matter of form declares
him baptized, in the name of Father, Son, and Holy
Spirit. Then the baptism proper follows: the elect
one baptizes the catechumen "*in thought, in word,
and in act*"—in his own intention, in the use of the

trinitarian formula, and in the corresponding threefold pouring of water—when the catechumen is
loosed from the bonds of Satan by the Father, is
inspired with the hope of salvation by the Son, and
is endued with love by the indwelling Spirit. As
after the ceremony of water-baptism the elect one
reads verses telling of Jesus' coming to the Jordan
to be baptized of John and of the latter's witness
to him (Matt. 3:13; Mark 1:9; Luke 3:21; John
1:29–34), so after the baptism proper he reads in
full the accounts of Christ's baptism and enduement
with the Spirit (Matt. 3:13–17; Mark 1:9–11;
Luke 3:21, 22), and the narrative of the gift of the
Spirit to the apostles (Acts 2:1–4), interspersing the
reading of these passages with prayers asking the
Father to seal the newly baptized in the "flesh and
blood" of his only begotten Son, the Son, to receive
them among his disciples, and to bestow upon them
the Spirit of his Father, and the Spirit, to come and
sanctify and dwell in them. This ritual, making
water-baptism, as it does, a prelude to a baptism in
Christ and an enduement with the Spirit of adoption,
is well summed up in that passage from Paul read
in connection with it which begins with the words:
"So that the law hath been our tutor to bring us unto
Christ, that we might be justified by faith. But now
that faith is come, we are no longer under a tutor.
For ye are all sons of God, through faith, in Christ
Jesus" (Gal. 3:24–29).

If the Paulicians regarded their baptism to be, as

a Christian sacrament, essentially a baptism by the Spirit, then we should expect them not to have been over-scrupulous about the symbolic form of it. And such we find to have been actually the case. Their regular mode of baptism, as we find it in the *Key*, is that combination of immersion and pouring which is known to be of very ancient origin in the Christian church. The candidate kneels in the water, and the elect one pours three handfuls of water on his head, severally in the name of the Father, and of the Son, and of the Holy Spirit. This mode was observed by two Paulician converts from Gumri who were baptized in a stream in the neighborhood of Arkhveli in 1837. But we have seen that the Paulicians of Gumri affirmed that according to Paulician teaching a handful of water was enough for baptism and in Arkhveli some were baptized in the same year from a bowl of water in a stable and in a private room.

We now come to the ordinal of the *Key*. The *Key* makes it the special duty of the elect one or minister of the church to examine the candidate for ordination, or, as the *Key* would say, election,

to see if he has perfect wisdom, love which is chief of all, discretion, meekness, humility, justice, courage, sobriety, and eloquence. Also whether he has continence, patience, administrative ability, fitness for the pastoral office, love of the poor, pity and good conduct of life, and all other good works, and repentance along with a keen conscience (pp. 39, 40).

At the ceremony of ordination the elect one presides,

but the rulers, or lay elders, are the ones to lay hands
upon the candidate.   At the beginning of the ceremony the candidate, whom the *Key* designates as
reader and *seeker*, receives an ordination name
"according to the gospel" (John 1:42; Matt. 16:
17, 18)—a usage which is in vogue also in the Gregorian church—after which "authority" is conferred
upon him by the elect one in these terms: "Receive
thou authority to bind and to loose the sons of men
in heaven and on earth" (p. 45).

It must not be supposed that the authority conferred upon the candidate for ordination placed any
priestly powers in his hands.   To the writer of the
Key oricular confession, priestly absolution, the
pretenses of popes and patriarchs and prelates, are
all an abomination.   The Paulician church had no
priesthood elevated above the people.   A characteristic clerical qualification laid down in the *Key*
is that the elect one shall be neither taller nor shorter
in stature than the average man.   Neither did the
Paulician church draw that hard and fast line between the clergy and the laity which the orthodox
churches drew.   The common believer received
the Spirit at his baptism; the elect one received the
Spirit for his special calling at his ordination.   Both
were said to be received into the number of Christ's
disciples.   And such a prayer as this in the ordinal,
"Establish thou this thine elect one in those works
which thou hast committed to all thine elect and to
all those who believe on thee" (p. 50), would seem

to indicate that the Paulicians after all believed in the apostleship of all Christians alike.[1]

The second half of the ordaining prayer is worth reproducing here. It was offered in concert by the elect one and the rulers, as they held their hands on high, and was addressed to Christ:

O thou life and refuge, mediator and intercessor, now head of things in heaven and on earth and under the earth, thou gate of heaven, the way of truth, and life unto those who rightly believe on thee, since thou didst promise with thy faithful word, "He who cometh unto me shall not remain in the darkness," and, "Him who cometh unto me I will not cast out," and forasmuch as this man who hath been baptized in thy holy name and hath been elected unto the Father in thy Holy Spirit, now awaits thy faithful promise, "Tarry ye in the city of Jerusalem until ye be endued with power from on high," we beseech thee, entreat thee, and pray thee, now falling down upon our faces at thy feet with fervent love and bitter tears, send into him the grace of thy Father, that it may come and adorn his spirit, mind, and body, and purify him from all evil thoughts; bestow upon him thy Spirit, which thou didst receive of the Father at the River Jordan, and strengthen thou him, and open, Lord, his mind, to understand the Scriptures and to take up the cross cheerfully and to come after thee now and ever and unto the eternities of eternities. Amen (pp. 46 f.).

At the close of the ordaining prayer the elect one breathed on the newly ordained minister thrice, saying: "May the breath of our Lord Jesus Christ open thy mind, my beloved son, and establish thee

[1] It was of a piece with this democratic view of the ministry that the Paulician church recognized no hierarchy, and believed strictly in the parity of the clergy (pp. 42 f.).

in thy works." The actual gift of the Holy Spirit was supposed to be received by a forty days' study of the New Testament under the elect one's direction, in imitation of the forty days which Christ spent in the wilderness.

Of sacraments the *Key of Truth* recognizes only three, namely, repentance, baptism or regeneration, and the communion of the body and blood of the Lord. When Christ said, "This is my body," the Spirit of the Father had actually changed the bread into his body, and it was for this that he gave thanks. The *Key* would also appear to teach some sort of transubstantiation effected by the elect one. For when Christ said explicitly, "This is *my* body," he had in mind the fact "that there were to come false popes who should change [the elements] according to their own good pleasure—who should deceive men with plain bread, or change it into their own body and blood *and not into those of Christ*" (p. 64). But such words as these should be taken with caution. They can hardly be given the weight of a deliberate statement of fact.

The calumny or ignorance of orthodox writers had led students of Paulicianism to believe that the Paulicians rejected the Old Testament and the writings of the apostle Peter. But we have seen that the Paulicians of Gumri spoke approvingly of the Decalogue. The story in Genesis of man's creation and fall is quoted in the *Key* as from the God-inspired Book; and we know from John of Otzoun, an Armenian writer of the eighth century, that the Paulicians quoted the prophets as authority. As to Peter, he is never spoken of disparagingly in the *Key*. On the contrary, his words are quoted as the words of a member of the Universal and Apostolic church. Only, it is affirmed that The Twelve, including Paul, are the Universal church, and not Peter alone.

We learn from the *Key* that the Paulicians did not call themselves Paulicians or Tonrakians, but, the Universal and Apostolic church. They, and not the orthodox churches, were the true church. To them, the orthodox churches, by turning baptism into a magic art, had apostatized from the faith, lost their orders, and forfeited their sacraments. As to the Mariolatry of those churches, and their adoration of saints and pictures and crosses, it was all nothing but idolatry. Says the *Key of Truth:*

Some have denied the precious mediation and intercession of the beloved Son of God, and have gone after the dead, and especially after pictures, stones, sticks, streams, trees, fountains, and all manner of other vain things, which, as they admit, they worship, offering to them incense and candles and sacrifices, all which is contrary to the Godhead—all which our Lord trampled under his holy feet when he said, "I am the door: by me if any man go in and out, he shall enter and shall find pasture" (pp. 53 f.).

The *Key of Truth* affords but meager material for a study of the polity of the Paulician church. But we may make an attempt to answer the question: Was the government of the Paulician church presbyterial in form? A presumption is established in

favor of an affirmative answer by the fact that the
sovereignty of the people seems to have been a recognized principle of government in the Paulician
church. In the ordinal of the *Key* the final responsibility of the ordination of a candidate is made to
rest with the people and their rulers (p. 44). Such
obscure expressions, also, of the orthodox Armenian
writers who speak of the Paulicians, as, "their self-
conferred contemptible priesthood" (Gregory of
Narek), and, "their outlandish election by
consent" (Gregory Magistros), are best explained
on the assumption that the power of ordination
in the Paulician church was vested in the lay
membership.

But our answer to the above question will in the
main depend on our view of the character of the
office of the Paulician *ruler*. Were the rulers of the
Key lay elders, or ordained presbyters? If they were
lay elders, the government of the Paulician church
was presbyterial. If they were ordained presbyters,
we have no evidence that the Paulician church had
in it any lay officers exercising authority in the
people's name. Professor Conybeare argues[1] that the
term for the spiritual authority of the ordained presbyter in both the Paulician and the orthodox Armenian church (*ishkhanoutioun*) is a derivative of the
term for ruler (*ishkhan*), and that, therefore, the
Paulician ruler must have been an ordained presbyter
or elect one. But an argument from the derivation

[1] *Introduction*, pp. cxxiv f.

of words in this case stands on no solid ground. In the modern orthodox Armenian church, indeed, while the priest's spiritual authority may be designated as *ishkhanoutioun,* the *ishkhank* are lay elders or trustees. For the following reasons the present writer prefers to believe that the ruler was a lay elder: (1) The two offices of elect one and ruler are clearly distinguished in the language of the *Key.* The elect one is the "elect one of Christ," a sort of vicar of Christ in the church, endued with his Spirit and vested with his mission on earth. The rulers represent the Universal and Apostolic church, and stand in the place of the apostles of Christ. The rulers and arch-rulers are also "elders." The elect one is also "teacher," "doctor," "primate," "bishop," "priest," "apostle," all of which terms are used interchangeably in the *Key.* But none of the names designating the pastoral office is used interchangeably with "ruler," "arch-ruler," or "elder." (2) In the ceremony of ordination the rulers identify themselves with the congregation and are so identified by the elect one (pp. 43, 44). The rulers bring the candidate before the elect one and ask him to ordain him in these words: "Holy father, falling down on our faces, we beseech, pray, and entreat thee with fervent love, to ordain this man *for the government of our souls.*" Then the elect one addresses the rulers in these words: "Now you who desire to have this man *as your shepherd,* have you proved him well, as I have proved him with much loving scrutiny?"

To which question of "the apostle of our Lord Jesus Christ" the rulers reply: "Yes, our excellent father; for all that thy lordship saith we have done by God's help." Then the elect one says *to the rulers and to all the hearers:* "I am free from responsibility in this matter, and yourselves only are responsible." (3) In the matter of the ruler's prerogatives a clear line is drawn at the sacraments, which would hardly be the case with an ordained presbyterate. The rulers examine a candidate for ordination with respect to his qualifications, and take an active part in the laying on of hands. But it is different with the rite of baptism. While the candidate for baptism is examined as to his faith "before the elect one and all the rulers" (p. 29), very much as he is examined before the church session of a modern Presbyterian church, it is expressly provided that none but an elect one shall administer that sacrament (p. 30).

Taking these different facts together, we may affirm with a fair degree of confidence, that the Paulician ruler was a lay elder, and, therefore, that the polity of the Paulician church was some form of presbyterianism. Beyond that general statement, however, we cannot venture; and what the difference was between rulers and arch-rulers we have no means of determining.

A faith rugged and puritanic on the eastern borders of the Roman empire, Paulicianism, once and again, sometimes by the daring and devotion of its votaries, sometimes by the impact of alien forces, was thrust upon the baptized paganism of the Greek world. But it bore more fruit in the western church than it did in the eastern. For the tenets of Paulicianism, planted in Thrace in the eighth and tenth centuries, spread into Poland and Bohemia, into Italy and France, into the countries of the Rhine, and even into far-off England, everywhere preparing the soil for the great Reformation which was to come.[1]

Nor were the Armenians to be left without a share in the blessings of that great awakening. In other chapters we shall see how the bread which they cast upon the waters after many days returned to them again.

In the nineteenth century Paulicianism in the East was replaced by Protestantism, and the latter now became what the former had of old been, pre-eminently an Armenian heresy. But Armenian Protestantism had a better lot than fell to the share of Armenian Paulicianism. The politico-religious world was much the same in the nineteenth that it had been in many preceding centuries: if the sultans of Turkey now played the part of the caliphs of Bagdad as the friends of iconoclasm, the tzars of Russia also played the part of the emperors of Byzantium as the champions of Greek orthodoxy. Yet it was

---

[1] See chap. liv of Gibbon, *History of the Decline and Fall of the Roman Empire*, and article "Pauliciani" in Smith and Wace, *Dictionary of Christian Biography*.

not quite the same: the Protestant powers of the West were now on the scene. And Armenian Protestantism received from them the strong political support for lack of which Armenian Paulicianism had well-nigh perished from the earth.

CHAPTER VI

THE FIRST REFORMERS

The first Protestant missionary societies to enter the Turkish empire were the Church Missionary Society of the Church of England, and the American Board of Commissioners for Foreign Missions. The former in 1815 sent a missionary to Egypt; the latter in 1818 assigned two men to Palestine.

The pioneers of the American Board in the Turkish empire early were impressed with the fact that the Armenians, of all the races in the Sultan's dominions, were the most open to Protestant missionary influences. In 1821 Parsons met at Jerusalem some Armenian pilgrims who showed him much cordiality, and led him to suggest to the Prudential Committee of the board the desirability of someone "making known to the churches the moral state of Armenia"— a suggestion which was to be carried out in 1833 by the publication of Smith and Dwight's *Researches*. Six years afterward—on New Year's Day, 1827— Bird and Goodell of the Syrian mission (established 1823) received two Armenian helpers, Bishop Dionysius and Vartabed Gregory, into the mission church at Beirut as the first-fruits of American missionary labors in Turkey. Such being the case there was nothing more natural than that the American Board and its missionaries should early be looking for an opportunity to do a special work for the Armenians of Turkey.

The temporary suspension of the Syrian mission created the desired opportunity. In May, 1828, the missionaries at Beirut and their Armenian helpers, finding their lives in danger from Mohammedan fanaticism aroused by the news of the battle of Navarino, sailed for the Island of Malta which sheltered the printing establishment of the mission of the Levant, and which, being a British possession, offered the fugitives a safe retreat from the political commotions of the times. The Syrian mission was for the time being abandoned, and the Syrian missionaries were given leisure for other work.

One of the first thoughts, naturally, was to put in operation the press which shortly before the arrival of the Beirut missionaries and in response to a recommendation made by them as early as 1824 had been sent to Malta for the purpose of printing literature exclusively for the Armenians (1827). Goodell immediately commenced to print some Armeno-Turkish tracts.[1] At the same time, with the help of Dionysius, he prosecuted the translation of the Armeno-Turkish Testament, until by January, 1830, this work was ready for the printer.[2]

[1] Tracts in the Turkish language printed in Armenian characters, intended for the use of Armenians whose vernacular was Turkish. About one-third of the Armenians of Turkey are said to belong to this class.

[2] Goodell's Armeno-Turkish Testament was not the first translation which made the Christian Scriptures intelligible to the Armenian laity. The Armeno-Turkish Testament of Keg-

In the meantime plans were maturing for the commencing of active missionary operations among the Armenians. A previous suggestion that Goodell might establish himself either at Smyrna or at Constantinople, "as his knowledge of Turkish will introduce him to the Armenians," took more definite shape in the year 1829 at a missionary conference convened at Malta by Rufus Anderson, assistant secretary of the American Board, at the time on a tour in the Levant, when it was proposed that Goodell should proceed to Constantinople and there establish a mission station; and pursuant to this recommendation, in the spring of 1831, Goodell received instructions from the Prudential Committee appointing him the first resident American missionary to the city of the Sultan.

William Goodell arrived at Constantinople on the

hamian of Erivan, published by the Russian Bible Society at St. Petersburg, had preceded it by nearly a decade (1822), and Zohrab's Modern Armenian Testament, published at Paris by the British and Foreign Bible Society, by six years (1825). These, however, had been rendered from the ancient Armenian Bible, while Goodell's version was the first to have the distinction of being made from the original Greek.

Goodell's life was largely devoted to the translation and repeated revision of the Armeno-Turkish Scriptures. His first translation of the New Testament was published in 1831; his first translation of the Old Testament, in 1842. He was assisted in the first by Bishop Dionysius; in the second, mainly by Panayotes Constantinides—a Greek who had been enlightened by intercourse with a certain Church of England clergyman, and who from 1835 to the time of his death in 1861 was Goodell's constant associate and helper. Goodell's Armeno-Turkish Bible was published in its final revised form in 1863—only two years before his last return to the United States, where he died (1867).

morning of June 9, 1831. H. G. O. Dwight joined him in the following year. Thus was founded the mission of the American Board to the Armenians of Turkey. In 1833, with their making the acquaintance of John Der-Sahakian, the work of these missionaries was launched.

Sahakian had formerly been a student at the patriarchal academy and a pupil of Peshtimaljian, the noted principal of that institution, and was one of those young Armenians of this time who were awakened to the superstitions of the church and earnestly desired its reformation, although at a loss as to what course to pursue to secure that end. When it was noised abroad in the city that two missionaries had come from America with the avowed object of establishing schools, but with the real purpose to spread infidelity, his curiosity was aroused, and, in January, 1833, he came to the mission, then in the suburb of Ortakeuy, on the Bosphorus, to ascertain the facts in the case for himself. The ultimate result was that in the summer of the same year (July 18) he came to place himself, with a companion, Minassian by name, under the instruction and guidance of the Americans who saw in the two young men the making of welcome interpreters of their message to the Armenian population of the city.[1]

[1] Sahakian was at this time private tutor in the home of an Armenian magnate. Minassian was a teacher in the patriarchal academy. The latter rendered the mission valuable service for

After a few months' work in Brousa, under the direction of the missionaries, Sahakian was in the fall of 1834 appointed general superintendent of the mission high school then recently opened (October 27, 1834) at Pera. This was the first school among the Armenians of Constantinople that offered such a variety of learning as eastern and western languages, with arithmetic, bookkeeping, geography, zoölogy, physics, astronomy, and theology. Alas, that it proved short-lived. The missionaries were careful from the beginning to disclaim all ulterior designs of proselytism in founding it; but the conservative element in the community looked upon it, nevertheless, with dire suspicion, and in a few years secured its suppression. Early in 1835 a priest was sent by the patriarch's vicar to inspect the school, and early in 1837, as soon, that is, as the imperial architects, Balian and Serverian, had set preparations on foot for the founding of a rival national college at Scutari, the parents of the students of the mission school were summoned before the vicar and ordered to withdraw their sons from the institution of the foreigners.

But the suppression of the mission school only transferred Sahakian to a post of yet wider influence. In the suburb of Hasskeuy on the Golden Horn the

a time, but in the end disappointed the missionaries by imbibing infidel ideas, of which, however, he is said to have repented before his death. He studied medicine in the United States, which may partly account for his relapse.

Armenians at this time had a large parish school—
one of the two or three foremost institutions of the
kind at the capital. Its patron, the famous Jezairlian, undertook early in 1837 to enlarge and to
remodel it on the Lancasterian plan, at this time
vigorously advocated by the missionaries, and placed
the very man whose activities the vicar had thought
to check by suppressing the mission school at the
head of this national institution to supervise the
making of the new changes. Sahakian willingly
accepted the call to Hasskeuy as affording a rare
opportunity for the spiritual work to which, with
him, everything else was but a means to an end, and
the more so as he was to be associated with a kindred
spirit in the person of the priest George Ardzrouni
who had been for some years a teacher in the school
at Hasskeuy. Endowed with great personal mag-
netism and boldness of speech, priest George,
although he never became a Protestant, was at this
time, both in school and parish, a most worthy representative of the evangelical cause; and as Sahakian
went to Hasskeuy, he knew that in his every effort
for religious enlightenment, he could depend on the
priest's hearty co-operation.

But Sahakian was not allowed long to remain at
Hasskeuy, any more than he was at Pera. Said
Dwight at the beginning of 1838, "The more I go
among the Armenians, the more evidence I see that
the work of the Lord has taken deep root in the
nation." But he added: "There are, however,

many watchful adversaries." And those watchful adversaries were more than Jezairlian cared to cope with. The school of Hasskeuy was for a time very popular. Six hundred scholars filled it to its utmost capacity. Jezairlian's example was soon followed by other magnates in the city and suburbs, and schools on the Lancasterian plan were established in Pera, Ortakeuy, and Psamatia. But by the end of 1838 the influence of the imperial architects, who bitterly opposed the countenancing of persons or ideas in any way associated with the missionaries, had compelled Jezairlian to dismiss his superintendent and to place his school on its former basis. The storms of persecution were already gathering about the evangelicals.

By this time, however, the evangelical movement had made considerable headway—so much headway, in fact, that the authorities of the church in their excitement estimated the evangelicals at about five hundred. Goodell had now for several years been conducting weekly meetings in Turkish for Bible-study and prayer. Dwight for over two years had been preaching in the Armenian tongue. The Evangelical Union, organized in 1836, a secret society, practically a church, now composed of about a score of members, had for three years been holding weekly meetings at the mission, and under the vigorous leadership of Sahakian, its secretary, had been making its influence felt both at the capital and in the provinces in the dissemination of evangelical ideas.

The imperial architects, engaged as they were in building one of the Sultan's favorite palaces, at this juncture had Mahmoud's ear, and consequently commanded the political power to push through almost any measure of their fancying in church and community. Conservative, and bigoted in their attitude toward the new sect, they now decided to resort to persecution. In maturing their persecuting schemes, their first step was to effect a change in the office of patriarchal vicar. The patriarch of the time, the amiable Stephen, surnamed "the Dove," had always been tolerant toward the missionaries, and in the earlier days of the mission had shown them much cordiality; and he did not approve of a persecution now. But he was a weak man, and could safely be ignored. The persecuting magnates felt that they only needed one in the office of vicar who could outdo in persecuting zeal the half-measures of the then incumbent to inaugurate the most thoroughgoing persecution. That one was found in Jacob Seropian, bishop of Marsovan and Amasia, who was brought to Constantinople on February 17, appointed patriarchal vicar, and vested with all the practical powers of the patriarchate.

When all plans had matured the persecution began in earnest. On February 19, 1839, Sahakian, the "ringleader" of the "evangelical infidels," and Paul Physica, another former pupil of Peshtimaljian's, who taught a school in the city in part supported by the mission, were arrested and cast into the patriarchal jail. Without a trial, or even a formal accusation, these men were on the fourth day of their confinement given in charge of a Turkish police officer, and by imperial edict hurried across Asia Minor into exile at the Convent of St. Garabed at Cesarea. The priest George was arrested in the following month in the same summary manner, and imprisoned for an entire month, after which he was exiled to the Convent of Armash, near Nicomedia. Several other ecclesiastics, altogether innocent of heresy, were at this time similarly treated. For the authorities were not very particular as to how many innocent ones suffered, provided the guilty were not allowed to go unpunished. On March 3 all missionary publications were by patriarchal bull put under the ban, and all those who were in possession of heretical books were called upon to deliver them up to their spiritual overseers. On March 25 Jacob, who had well vindicated the confidence which the imperial architects had reposed in him, was allowed to supplant Stephen in the patriarchal chair. Stephen retired to the Convent of Armash, his episcopal seat near Nicomedia, and presently an imperial edict followed directing the patriarchs of the several Christian sects "to look well to their flocks, and guard them against foreign influence and infidelity." On April 28 the new patriarch issued a bull, even more violently worded than the preceding one, threatening terrible anathemas against all those who should be found having any intercourse with the

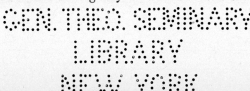

missionaries or reading their books, and against all such as should neglect to inform on offenders.

Even more than the persecution of individual natives the object upon which the persecutors had set their heart was the expulsion of the American missionaries from the country. And the personnel of the diplomatic corps at this juncture seemed in its character highly favorable to their attaining their object. Commodore Porter, the American *chargé d'affaires*, who was personally very friendly to the missionaries, not only was an envoy of secondary rank, but entertained a view of the Turkish-American Treaty of 1830 which allowed of no American missionary proselytism in the Turkish empire.[1] Lord Ponsonby, the British ambassador, although a Protestant, was totally absorbed in matters of diplomacy, and was no friend of missionaries. The Dutch, Swedish, and Prussian legations were temporarily in charge of Roman-Catholic subordinates, who along with the representatives of the Roman-

[1] On May 16, 1841, in reply to a note from the Porte requesting the removal of the American missionaries from the Lebanon, Mr. Porter wrote: "The Constitution of the United States allows to all its citizens the right of the free exercise of their religious opinions, but no article of the Treaty of Commerce and Navigation between the United States and Turkey gives them authority to interfere in any way with the rites and religion of any person living under the authority of Turkey. Therefore, after this correspondence has been made known to the American citizens residing in the vicinity of Mount Lebanon, any attempt to excite the minds of the inhabitants to change their rites and religion, must be done at their own risk, and on their responsibility."

Catholic powers were as eager as the Armenian hierarchy to have Protestantism driven out of the country. As to the Russian Ambassador Boutineff, inflexible enemy that he was of the missions of the American Board in Turkey, he openly declared to one of the American missionaries, "My lord, the Tzar of Russia, will never allow Protestantism to set its foot in Turkey."[1]

But this the first organized persecution of Protestants in Turkey collapsed in the twinkling of an eye. Sultan Mahmoud died on July 1, and the persecuting magnates lost their imperial support. At the same time Ibrahim Pasha's invasion of Asia Minor brought the arms and diplomacy of Protestant England into the forefront, and crowded the influence of orthodox Russia out of the Ottoman divan. About the middle of August the Armenian magnates decided to arrest the persecution. The exiles were told to return home—Sahakian, the last of them, returning to Constantinople in the May of 1840—and on September 27 Stephen again came to power and popu-

---

[1] It is well known that it was by order of Ambassador Boutineff that a Russian Armenian by the name of Taliatian, in the employ of the American mission at Constantinople as instructor to Cyrus Hamlin, was one day in May, 1839, suddenly seized and placed on board a steamer bound for Trebizond, to be banished to Siberia. Hamlin relates (*Among the Turks*, pp. 34–37) how Taliatian landed at Trebizond with an American passport, and found his way to Calcutta, where he was to distinguish himself as an author and as the editor of *The Patriot*. Taliatian was a native of Erivan, a deacon in the Armenian church, and a former pupil of Bishop Heber at Bishop's College, Calcutta.

larity. Then followed a great reaction in public sentiment, and the evangelical cause once more advanced apace.

This period of the evangelical movement is closely associated with the name of Gregory Peshtimaljian, the famous principal of the patriarchal academy. The reform movement in the Armenian church before the year 1839 owed its existence in large measure to this man's influence. It is a noteworthy fact that all of the first reformers and many of the later had, at one time or another, sat at his feet.

Peshtimaljian was for his day a man of wide learning and literary attainments. He was a religious poet of no mean ability, and the author of several important educational works. He was well versed in church history, both oriental and occidental, and held a high rank among the theologians and biblical scholars of his community. When, therefore, the patriarchal academy at Koom-kapou, originally founded by the patriarch Jacob Nalyan, and destroyed by the fire of 1826, was reopened in 1829 through the munificence of Haroutioun Bezjian and his coadjutors, Peshtimaljian, who had been teaching in the parish school of Ortakeuy, was thought of as the best man for such a responsible place, and was appointed principal of the institution. In this school of learning some fifty scholars, who composed the most advanced of four classes, studied grammar and logic under Peshtimaljian's immediate supervision. It was Peshtimaljian's duty also as principal of the academy to instruct all candidates

for the priesthood, who, according to regulations
lately adopted by the Synod of the patriarchate,
could not be ordained to the sacred office without
first having pursued a prescribed course of study
in that institution. Thus in the course of his daily
routine, Peshtimaljian had ample opportunity to
instil in the minds of his pupils, both clerical and
lay, a good deal of Christian truth, the more readily
as the ancient Armenian New Testament was one
of the important textbooks used in language-study.
That his teaching could have been marked by much
spirituality is not to be supposed; but how little
sympathy he had with the formalism of the church
may be inferred from one of his sayings in criticism
of the day's orthodoxy: "When God created man,
he made him in his own image; but man has now
reversed the order, and endeavors to make God in
man's image."

All classes of men loved Peshtimaljian; but when
he died none, perhaps, missed him more than the
evangelicals who had looked upon him as the best
friend that they had in the church. For while
Peshtimaljian looked sometimes with dismay upon
what he considered to be foolish radicalism on the
part of the missionaries and their youthful followers,
at this early stage of the Armenian reformation
there was no measure to which he could not
ultimately be reconciled. Peshtimaljian never saw
the evangelical movement come to a crisis, and
was never called upon to take a decided stand for

it. He died in January, 1838, at the age of sixty-four years.

The beginnings of the evangelical movement in the city of Nicomedia are contemporaneous with its beginnings at Constantinople. In the year 1832, Goodell went on an overland tour to Brousa, preparatory to the establishment of a mission station in that city. On his way thither he spent a day in Nicomedia, where he visited the Armenian church, distributed a few Armeno-Turkish tracts at the church door, and left with an old priest a copy of his Armeno-Turkish New Testament. This led, so far as our information goes, to the awakening in Nicomedia. An Armeno-Turkish translation of Legh Richmond's *The Dairyman's Daughter* was among the tracts distributed, and it was especially the means of inculcating a spiritual religion and rousing an interest in the searching of the Scriptures. Kit Varjabed was at this time the principal of the parish school in Nicomedia, which like other parish schools was situated within the precincts of the church. He soon gathered around himself a company of priests and laymen, who daily met in a room within the church inclosure for the study of the Scriptures. In 1838 the band numbered sixteen souls. The fundamental doctrines of the gospel—so we are told by the missionaries who visited them—were very clearly apprehended by these men, and an earnest spirituality was their distinctive mark. When the ex-patriarch Stephen returned to his diocese in 1839, persecution was on the point of breaking out against the "Christian Brethren," as they were called among themselves, but the presence of that primate restrained the bigotry of their enemies, and the little band was suffered to grow unmolested. Thus without the help of a resident missionary began in Nicomedia a movement which soon spread into the surrounding country, and before long gave to the evangelical cause in general one of its best workers in the person of the priest Vertanes.

CHAPTER VII

THE PROTESTANT EXCISION

The reaction in public sentiment which followed the persecution of 1839 made it possible for the American missionaries to renew their efforts with redoubled vigor. In the November of 1840 the mission high school was reopened at Bebek on the Bosphorus, under the supervision of Cyrus Hamlin who had arrived at Constantinople in the January of the preceding year. In 1840 over six, and in the following year over five million pages of the Scriptures and religious literature in Armenian and Armeno-Turkish were printed at the mission press at Smyrna, and sent to points as far apart as Adrianople and Odessa, Adabazar, Cesarea, and Tiflis. Before the end of 1840 Dwight rented in a khan in the business quarter of Stamboul an office where twice every week he met with inquirers on religion, at the same time that he conducted at the mission a service every Sunday and two week-day inquiry meetings every week. Dwight's meetings of inquiry rapidly gained in popularity. The total number of those who at various times attended them rose from a score to a hundred and twenty and more. Those attending the meetings belonged for the most part to the middle class, who were the freest from the trammels of worldliness on the one hand and of bigotry on the other—the class which Protestantism has won as well as developed in the Turkish empire.

Thus the new ideas spread, and began to make a great stir. Everywhere the tone of religious feeling appeared to be changing. The clergy sought more and more in the Bible the topics for their public discourses. In public places at the capital, such as coffee shops and bazars, the new doctrines were freely discussed. Brousa, the most unpromising field of the whole mission, began to give enough signs of promise to justify the missionaries, on the point of being ordered to some other field, to continue their stay in that city; while in the diocese of Marsovan and Amasia, over which presided the persecuting ex-patriarch Jacob, missionary literature was freely circulated. It is true that the accession of Theodore to the patriarchal chair on October 1, 1841, became the signal for a revival of persecuting zeal, which continued more or less throughout his reign. Still, persecution never assumed formidable proportions under Theodore's reign, and early in 1844, such had been the progress of the evangelical movement in the meantime, Goodell, while anticipating much serious opposition calculated to retard its further progress, could use in addressing the "brethren" at Constantinople the following sanguine words: "If this work of God go forward for ten years to come as it has gone for ten years past, there will be no further occasion for any of us [missionaries] to remain here; unless it be to assist you in bringing

to a knowledge of these same precious saving doctrines of the gospel, the Greeks and Jews, and others
around you."

But the greatest persecution was yet to come under
the patriarch Matthew, formerly bishop of Brousa
and late of Smyrna, who ascended the patriarchal
chair on July 29, 1844. As a premonition of the
coming storm, Matthew in the latter part of that
year instructed all parish priests to keep a record of
the names of all those who failed to come to the
confessional at the appointed seasons.

Unruffled, however, by the gathering clouds of
persecution, the evangelicals at Constantinople
made this a time of unusual missionary activity, and
many of them set out to preach in distant cities and
villages the doctrines of the Protestant reformation.
One man visited the towns south of the Marmora;
another went eastward in Asia Minor as far as Trebizond; still another proceeded to Varna, while two
went together on a missionary tour in European
Turkey through Rodosto, Salonika, Philippi, Adrianople, Philippopolis, and Sophia.

The missionaries who superintended this work
had themselves by this time cast aside all their former
reserve, and now stood out in the eyes of the public
as the great heresiarchs, and the chief leaders of the
evangelical movement. Matthew on his accession
earnestly recommended it to some evangelicals that
waited on him that the Americans might proceed
with great caution, and not make themselves con-

spicuous before the public; but such a course, heartily indorsed and pursued by the missionaries themselves at the beginning of their operations, did not longer "seem to be practicable." Toward the end of 1844 Matthew lodged the complaint directly with the missionaries that their work was attracting more of the public notice than was desirable, and inquired how long they proposed to remain in Turkey. Goodell made this reply to the patriarch's messenger:

Let there be so many and so good schools established in the nation, that ours shall not only cease to attract attention, but shall become unnecessary and be wholly forsaken.

Let there be so much and so good preaching in all the various churches that no one will ever think of coming again to hear us stammer in a foreign tongue.

Should he, or any other person, again ask how long we are going to stay, and how much longer they will have to bear with us, show them Isa. 6:11, 12, and say that when the prophet asked, "how long" he should prophesy, the Lord said, "Till the land be an utter desolation, and the inhabitants be removed far away;" but that we, by the grace of God, were going to stay and prophesy till the land should be greatly blessed, and the people brought very nigh and made very happy as "heirs of God, and joint-heirs with Christ."[1]

Just before resorting to violent measures Matthew had recourse to public debate. A number of private discussions had been held at Hasskeuy in the homes of various magnates in the spring and early summer of 1845, in which Tschamourjian (Deroyentz), later principal of the national college at Scutari, and

[1] *Missionary Herald*, April, 1845, p. 113.

Hatschadourian, later pastor of the first evangelical church of Constantinople, had figured prominently as the spokesmen respectively of the church and of the reform party. These private discussions, while they had early been suppressed by the patriarch, had rendered imperative some show of reasonableness on the part of the champions of the church's orthodoxy. In November, therefore, Tschamourjian was directed to conduct public discussions at the patriarchate, and to publish two pamphlets, one discussing the church's doctrine of baptismal regeneration, and another the church's doctrine of transubstantiation.

Tschamourjian's pamphlets, however, like the public lectures which he delivered at the patriarchate on two successive Sundays, defeated their object by challenging a reply. The first of them was answered by the missionary Wood, the second by Hatschadourian. One passage from the latter's tract is here quoted to illustrate the kind of argument that was now being used, and to show how open controversy had at this time taken the place of quiet gospel teaching:

In the very words used at the institution of the sacrament of the communion, Christ clearly declares his object in establishing it, when he says, "This do in remembrance of me." He does not say, "This do in sacrifice of me," nor, "This do for the pardon of the sins of the living and the dead." These are things which *you* add to the words of Christ. Christ appointed this ordinance, that it should remain in his church *in remembrance* of his sacrifice. We read, "As oft as ye eat this bread, and drink this cup, ye do show the Lord's death till he come" (I Cor. 11:26). The apostle says, "ye do show the Lord's death;" but *you* understand him to say, "ye do sacrifice the Lord." Christ says, "This do in remembrance of me;" but *you* understand him to say, "This do in order to manufacture me."[1]

Seeing that expostulation and argument alike were of no avail, Matthew finally addressed himself to the task of suppression. More than one consideration seemed in favor of a persecution at this time. By the year 1846 it had been definitely ascertained that the numerical strength of the evangelical party was not great. The numbers of the reformers, formerly exaggerated by popular alarmists to some eight thousand, had been found to amount at most to a few hundred, and this number had further been reduced by the desertion in view of persecution of such friends of ecclesiastical reform as had been enlightened in their minds but had not been quickened in their consciences. In the second place, Horatio Southgate, missionary bishop of the American Episcopal church at Constantinople—a foreigner and a fellow-countryman of the other missionaries— made no secret of his sympathy for Matthew's plans of intolerance. Himself a ritualistic Episcopalian, the bishop regarded the evangelicals as rebels against the patriarch's apostolic succession, and their ideas as nothing but "a mixture of radicalism and infidelity," and when Matthew was considering the

[1] *Reply to the First Pamphlet of the Treatise on the Communion*, pp. 46 ff.

subject of anathema and excision, he encouraged
him to adopt "reasonably coercive measures."
Indeed, after the persecution of Protestants had begun
"he labored with all his might to make the British
ambassador believe that there was no persecution
going on, but that only church discipline was being
administered, with which no one ought to interfere."[1]
That the see of Etschmiadzin also had a direct hand
in the persecution which Matthew inaugurated, as
Cyrus Hamlin firmly believed,[2] is not at this day
easily decided; but this one thing is certain that the
ecclesiastical relations of the patriarchate of Constantinople to that see, suspended through the jeal-
ousy of the Turkish government since the trans-
ference of the territory about Etschmiadzin to Russia
(1828), were restored only two months after Matthew's accession.

The patriarchal anathema first fell upon Vertanes
Eznak Krikorian, commonly known as the priest
Vertanes, who was at this time the most indefatigable
and influential of the reformers.[3] But before we
relate the circumstances of his excommunication
it will be well for us to review briefly the antecedent
career of the man.

The priest Vertanes was in the service of the church
of Nicomedia when he attached himself to the little

[1] *Autobiography of William G. Schauffler*, p. 188.

[2] *My Life and Times*, p. 284.

[3] Sahakian was at this time in America, receiving a theological
education.

band of Bible readers that began to form in that city in 1832. Clerical opposition at Nicomedia compelled him in the spring of 1838 to go to Yenikeuy on the Bosphorus where a former associate, the priest Haroutioun (of whom we shall see more later), had preceded him toward the end of 1836. Stephen, who was then the reigning patriarch, and, as former bishop of the diocese of Nicomedia, an old acquaintance of the priests, repaired to the same village in the summer of that year; and the reformation of the Armenian church was often made by these men the subject of conversation, the patriarch heartily entering into the discussion, and even declaring "that many observances in their church were not Christianity, and that they would not probably exist ten years longer." In this secluded village Vertanes spent nearly two and one-half quiet years, unnoticed during the persecution of 1839, officiating in the village church, and often meeting with Panayotes (Goodell's Greek assistant) and Haroutioun for prayer.

In 1840 Vertanes removed his residence to the city (the Mousallah quarter of Stamboul), the priest Haroutioun continuing a while longer at Yenikeuy before returning to his home in Nicomedia. In that year began for Vertanes a ministry extending over a period of many years, performed sometimes under the direction of the mission, sometimes independently, until his death in 1875, at the ripe age of eighty-seven years. From house to house and from shop to shop, wherever he could gain a hearing, Vertanes preached the doctrine of justification by faith. His office of confessor, also, gave him access to the women whom neither lay evangelist nor missionary could reach, and many an illiterate woman received from him her first lessons in the Bible.

Nor was Vertanes' mission confined to the capital. In two successive years, 1841 and 1842, he had occasion to visit Nicomedia and vicinity, and in 1843, Asia Minor and Armenia. This last missionary tour so irritated the patriarch Theodore that Vertanes was arrested on his return to Constantinople and exiled (December, 1843) to the Convent of Armash. Here, however, under the mild indifference of Stephen who had preceded him to the convent, he exerted such an influence over the inmates as to cause serious alarm at headquarters, and when Matthew succeeded to the patriarchal throne he was further exiled (February, 1845) to the Convent of St. Garabed at Cesarea. But Vertanes' presence proved not less dangerous to orthodoxy at Cesarea than it had been at Armash. Nine years afterward a missionary, writing on the occasion of the establishment of a mission station and the organization of a Protestant church in the city, said: "The seeds of reformation were sown here years ago, when bitter persecution banished the devoted Vertanes to this city. We have seen some of the fruits of his labors, and hope to see many more. They banished the man, but not his religion. So great was his zeal that they were glad to recall him, lest all the Armenians should become Protestants."

In August, 1845, Vertanes was permitted to return to Constantinople by virtue of a general amnesty proclaimed on the occasion of the anniversary of the Sultan's accession to the throne, and thus it came that he was at the capital when the storm of 1846 burst upon the evangelicals. On January 23, 1846, one of the patriarch's beadles was ordered, with the chief municipal officer of the quarter of the city where Vertanes had his lodgings, to go and arrest the arch-heretic and to bring him before the supreme ecclesiastical authority. Vertanes, however, received warning in time to flee to Dwight's house in Pera, and the patriarch was cheated of a much-coveted opportunity to read the bull of excision and anathema in his hearing and to go through the solemn form of publicly divesting him of his priestly robes. On Sunday, January 25, at the close of the morning services, and before mass, the candles of the patriarchal church were extinguished, the great screen was drawn before the high altar, and a solemn bull of excision and anathema was read against Vertanes and all the "modern sectaries." In this document Matthew declared Vertanes a "wretched and unworthy" priest who,

following his carnal lusts, leaves the church and his sacred office, and, like a vagabond, going about through the metropolis and Nicomedia, babbles our errors, unworthy of his sacred office and dignity, and becomes an occasion of stumbling to many; and altogether throwing aside the holiness of faith, which he had received in the holy Catholic Armenian church, follows the erroneous doctrines of modern sectaries, and begins to preach errors in Nicomedia, Cesarea, Anatolia, and in Constantinople, and in every place where he sets his impious foot, and to overwhelm the simple people in spiritual destruction.

After speaking of the priest's obstinacy in not hearkening to the good counsels of his lordship, and of the danger to the spiritual welfare of his flock involved in the free access to the community of such "a traitor and murderer of Christ," the patriarch concluded:

Wherefore we expel him, and forbid him as a devil, and a child of the devil, to enter into the company of our believers; we cut him off from the priesthood by the Word of God as an amputated member of the spiritual body of Christ, and as a branch cut off from the vine, which is good for nothing, but to be cast into the fire. By this admonitory bull I, therefore, command and warn my beloved in every city, far and near, not to look upon his face, regarding it as the face of Belial; not to receive him into your holy dwellings, for he is a house-destroying and ravening wolf; not to receive his salutation, but as a soul-destroying and deadly poison; and to beware, with all your households, of similar seducing and impious followers of the false doctrine of modern sectaries, and to pray for them to the God who remembereth not iniquity, if, perchance, they may repent, and turn from their wicked ways, and find the salvation of their souls, through the grace of our Lord and Savior Jesus Christ, who is blessed world without end. Amen.[1]

[1] For the full text of this bull in the original see Berberian, *Armenian History*, pp. 299 ff. The English translation is given in the *Missionary Herald*, June, 1846, pp. 196 f., and Dwight, *Christianity Revived in the East*, pp. 267 ff.

One after another during the week that followed the excision of Vertanes, the evangelicals were called up by the patriarch and required to sign, on pain of excommunication, a paper of recantation, declaring that "being deceived by the wicked enticements of Satan," they had withdrawn from the fellowship of the "holy Armenian church," and had been "caught in the loose and soul-destroying doctrines of the new sectaries;" affirming "that the faith of the holy church is spotless, her sacraments divine, her rites of apostolic origin, her ritual pious;" and renouncing all further intercourse with the "new sectaries."[1]

During the first week following the excision of Vertanes none of the evangelicals affixed his signature to this document, and on the following Sunday Matthew issued a more emphatic anathema. His holiness again warned the pious against all those who harbored the sentiments of Vertanes in such terms as these:

Whoever has a son that is such a one, or a brother, or a partner [in business], and gives him bread, or assists him in making money, or has intercourse with him as a friend, or does business with him, let such persons know that they are nourishing a venomous serpent in their houses, which will one day injure them with its deadly poison, and they will lose their souls. Such persons give bread to Judas. Such persons are enemies of the holy faith of Christianity, and

[1] *Reply to the First Manifesto Published against the Evangelical Christians*, pp. 19 ff.; *Christianity Revived in the East* pp. 272 ff.

destroyers of the holy orthodox Armenian church, and a disgrace to the whole nation. Wherefore, their houses and shops are also accursed; and whoever goes to visit them, we shall learn and make them public in the holy church by terrible anathema.[1]

On February 3 the evangelicals addressed an appeal to the patriarch. In this appeal they stated that they were not infidels or heretics as they had been called, but true believers in the gospel which the church herself receives. They made a brief declaration of their faith, professing their belief in the Trinity, in the Holy Spirit, and in the Lord Jesus Christ, "the only Savior of the world, and true High Priest, Mediator, and Intercessor for believers;" in the Scriptures of the Old and New Testaments, as "the perfect rule of the church;" in baptism in the name of the Trinity, and in the Lord's Supper "in commemoration of the death of our Lord." Finally they declared their acceptance of the Nicene Creed as the symbol of faith adopted by the entire church of Christ, and concluded:

Thus, for our not receiving things not plainly taught in the Holy Scriptures, esteeming it obstinacy and rebellion, will you call us enemies of our nation and destroyers of our church? We have no such design; but, in accordance with what Paul wrote to the Romans (Rom. 9:3), we love our nation to such a degree that we glory in being called Armenians; and we by no means acknowledge any other name, although we are commonly called Protestants. But we again declare that we are Armenians by nation, Christians by faith, and

[1] *Missionary Herald*, June, 1846, p. 198; *Christianity Revived in the East*, pp. 270 f.

obedient subjects of the Ottoman government. Nevertheless, if in religious or civil matters we be in error—for we do not claim to be infallible—we will gladly admit it, if you will deign to point out our error to us. You well know that the conviction of the human mind is effected only by the presentation of truth, not by the exercise of force; and in the fear of God we can do nothing against our conscience.[1]

Lithographed copies of this appeal were scattered broadcast in the community. This was an epoch-making document. It raised the first clear protest ever heard in Turkey against religious intolerance. In view of that protest, if for no other cause, the evangelicals might have been called by the name which in this very document they repudiated—Protestants.

But the appeal went unheeded. From week to week the patriarchal anathemas thundered from the churches of the metropolis. Every Lord's Day some recalcitrant evangelicals who had refused to sign the paper of recantation were anathematized and exscinded by name. In the course of four weeks about thirty were thus cast out of the church and delivered up to Satan. The first paper of recantation being thought too vague or conciliatory in its phraseology, it was replaced in the middle of February by another document commonly known as the "New Creed" of the patriarch Matthew. For the purpose of eliminating every person who held the evangelical doctrines nothing better could have been

[1] *Reply to the First Manifesto Published against the Evangelical Christians*, pp. 2 ff.; *Missionary Herald*, June, 1846, pp. 197 f.

devised. It required assent to the following points: (1) Faith without works cannot save a man; and the proof of the correctness of a Christian's faith is not his good works, but the conformity of his confession to the creed of the universal church. (2) The visible church under the headship of Christ and the guidance of the Holy Spirit "never has erred and never can err." (3) The sacraments of the church are seven in number, namely, baptism, confirmation, penance, communion, ordination, matrimony, and extreme unction. (4) Ceremonial baptism is essential to salvation, and the unbaptized person "is out of the church, and has no salvation, even though he had never sinned at all;" confession to a priest with true repentance, and submission to the penance imposed by him, are indispensable to forgiveness and "eternal glory;" and the souls of such as die before having performed full penance for sins committed must be purified by the prayers of the church, the sacrifice of the mass, and the giving of special alms, to become worthy of "eternal glory." (5) "The mystery of the holy communion is the true body and blood of Christ," and "whoever does not partake of the communion in this belief is under eternal condemnation." (6) The Virgin is "Mother of God," perpetually a virgin, and "worthy of honor above all the saints;" "the intercession of the saints is acceptable to God, and their relics and anointed pictures are worthy of veneration;" and "the holy cross and the relics of saints" are unfailing instruments of God's wonder-working power. (7) "To believe in the church means, to believe those things which the universal holy church of Christ unitedly believes, and to believe them in the same way in which she believes." The true follower of the church must observe "her external ceremonies of piety and Christian rites, and all her requirements, as having been received by tradition from the holy apostles, and the holy fathers who came after them." (8) There are different grades of office in the church; and the patriarchs of every nation "are Christ's vicegerents, appointed to shepherd the holy church, and to superintend her discipline." (9) Those who declare that "error has entered into the faith unitedly received by the universal church," affirming the "Mother of God" to be only "Mother of Christ," and denying her perpetual virginity; condemning the veneration of the "holy cross," the relics of saints, and anointed pictures, as idolatry, and denying the intercession of saints, are anathema, "as impious blasphemers of the Holy Spirit, and enemies of God and all his saints."[1]

From the day following the excommunication of Vertanes, clergy and laity were intent upon putting down the heretics, and persecution began in earnest. Under the then organization of the trades in Turkey ecclesiastical discipline was a very effective means of civil oppression. All the various trades at Con-

[1] *Reply to the First Manifesto Published against the Evangelical Christians*, pp. 22 ff.; *Christianity Revived in the East*, pp. 274 ff.

stantinople, as also in other large towns in Turkey,
were in those days incorporated guilds, and the affairs
of each guild were administered by a committee
consisting of the wealthiest and most influential
members of it. This committee, whose powers
were often vested in a single individual known as
the clerk of the guild, issued all licenses to trade
upon the surety of one or more of the most important
licensed tradesmen of the guild. The patriarchal
anathema, by forbidding all intercourse between
"the pious" and the "new sectaries," deprived the
evangelicals of their surety and thereby withdrew
their licenses to trade. About thirty-five men thus
forfeited their licenses, and in consequence some of
them were cast into jail, and some were compelled
to make immediate settlement of their accounts with
partners and creditors, incurring great financial loss.

But the commercial boycott was not all that the
ban entailed. The ban involved also social ostra-
cism, which was something of which the civil power
could not take cognizance, and which therefore
lasted for a much longer period than the other.
Nearly seventy individuals at Constantinople were
by virtue of the patriarchal anathema driven from
their homes and forced to separate from father,
mother, brother, sister, husband, wife, or child,
refused food or shelter, robbed, insulted, and injured
by their own and by every Christian sect in the city.
Goodell thus described the condition of the evangelicals in the middle of March:

Many are driven from their homes, and denied a shelter or a drop of water from any sect; refused a place to live in, a place to die in, or a place to be buried in; unable to flee to a mountain or a cave for want of a passport; unable to work, for whoever employs them shares their fate; thrown into the filthiest prisons for want of security, and whoever offers himself for security is thrown in with them.[1]

But foreign sympathy came to the rescue of the evangelicals in the hour of their dire distress. The missionaries secured for them tenements where they found temporary shelter; and there they were cared for during the first months of the persecution by the contributions of Protestant sympathizers in England and America, in India and the Caucasus, in Denmark and Sweden and Norway, in Würtemberg and Switzerland. Thus brought together by a common tribulation and a universal philanthropy, many of them hitherto total strangers to each other, they shared together their common trials and their common joys. Goodell's words give us an insight into the manner in which they bore up under their affliction:

They had days of public fasting and prayer, and the spectacle was an affecting one. Their songs of praise from the whole congregation went up like the sound of many waters, and reminded me of the singing of the ancient Bohemian brethren amidst the raging fires of persecution. And, indeed, to see them stand from day to day with such firmness on the Rock of eternal ages, unmoved and undismayed; to see them manifest such unshaken confidence in the power and wisdom and faithfulness of Christ; to see them take

[1] *Memoirs*, pp. 312 f.

joyfully the spoiling of their goods, knowing that they have in heaven a better and an enduring substance; to see them called up, one after another, from time to time, even women and children, and going alone, single-handed, cheerfully and fearlessly, into the presence of the greatest and craftiest of their enemies, and there witnessing a good confession, to the utter confusion of their inquisitors—was a spectacle for angels and for men.[1]

Surely the noble words which one of the evangelicals at this time uttered voiced a sentiment which they all felt in common: "My daily prayer to God is, that even if there should not be left a single person except myself to witness for the truth, He would still give me faith to stand firm for the doctrine of salvation by grace in Christ alone. I know that all the resistance we now make to error we are making for coming generations."

Meanwhile the evangelicals were not helplessly idle. In the middle of February they sent in a petition to Reshid Pasha, minister of foreign affairs, refuting all charges of civil rebellion, pointing out the reason for their persecution as lying in their refusal to conform themselves to some usages of the national church like the worship of images and priestly absolution, and begging for the protection of the imperial government.[2] In the following month they submitted a petition to the British, Prussian, and American diplomatic representatives, and finally one to the Sultan himself. At last, on March

[1] *Memoirs*, p. 311.

[2] See *Missionary Herald*, June, 1846, pp. 198 f.

12, Reshid Pasha summoned the patriarch to the Porte for an interview, with the result that Matthew publicly declared from the pulpit of the cathedral church: "Religion is free in Turkey!" And on May 17 the evangelicals were called up by the prefect of the police and informed that they were now authorized to resume their occupations and that their surety for each other would be deemed sufficient. The "vizierial letter" which authorized them, in the name of the Sultan, to open their shops, gave them that right as "Protestants." From this time forward the evangelicals were to be officially known by that name. This vizierial letter caused a cessation of all civil persecution of Protestants at Constantinople. At the same time it was the entering wedge for their civil emancipation.

The patriarch's "New Creed" went to the provinces at the same time that it was issued at the capital. At Nicomedia, Adabazar, Brousa, Smyrna, Trebizond, and Erzroom, the same document was submitted to the evangelicals for their signatures, and a refusal to comply was there, as it was at Constantinople, followed by the ban and the anathema. Persecution in the provinces was not less thoroughly organized than at the capital; and it often operated with greater severity because foreign interference was not easily obtained. Brousa and Smyrna,[1] in

[1] The mission station at Brousa was established in 1834 originally for the Greek population of the city; that at Smyrna was established in the year preceding, when the mission press at Malta was removed thither.

each of which two places four evangelicals were excommunicated, present the only exceptions to this general rule. At these two points no persecution was attempted.

We will take a rapid survey of events in the four other localities.

In the city of Trebizond, where a mission station had been established in 1835, nine were excommunicated. For many months after the anathema the evangelicals were subject to mob violence and imprisonment on false charges.

In the interior city of Erzroom, where a mission station had been established in the latter part of 1839, six were excommunicated. Here there were some fierce outbursts of mob violence. A vizierial letter, however, dated June 2, 1846, notified the pasha of Erzroom that persecution was no longer to be tolerated. It was the will of his imperial majesty the Sultan, with regard to those of his Armenian subjects who had embraced the Protestant faith, that "the patriarch should be forbidden to interfere in their religious or personal affairs; and that all concerned, when sureties were offered by them from among the various communities, should accept them; and that thus there should be no hindrance to their pursuing their occupations and gaining their living."[1] After the evangelicals of Constantinople, those of Erzroom were the first thus to receive government protection.

[1] *Missionary Herald*, September, 1846, p. 302.

In Adabazar[1] the evangelicals suffered persecution at the hands of the ecclesiastical authorities in the winter of 1844–45; and when in 1846 orders came from the patriarchate to renew the persecution, mob violence also became common. But when in the latter part of July the arrival of a missionary occasioned renewed disturbance in the town and the evangelicals were arraigned before the kadi for intercourse with the foreigner, their declaration that they were Armenians by nationality, evangelical Christians by faith, and loyal subjects of the Ottoman Porte, elicited this answer from that dignitary: "We cannot interfere with your excommunication; but so long as you abide by the declaration you have now made, we will protect you civilly. Your goods shall be as our goods, your houses as our houses, and your persons as our persons. Go in peace." On the following day, Sunday, July 26, twenty-four of the evangelicals in the town were excommunicated by name. On the same night an evangelical church was organized in Adabazar.

In Nicomedia twelve of the evangelicals were prevailed upon by the ex-patriarch Stephen to sign the "New Creed," the bishop declaring that he only wanted their signatures "as a matter of form." Soon, however, a missionary visitor came to Nicome-

---

[1] The evangelical movement at Adabazar originated from the gift of a New Testament in modern Armenian and a few tracts by Dwight and Hamlin to a certain native of that town, Erizian by name, on a visit to Nicomedia in the summer of 1840.

dia. He urged upon them what he deemed to be their duty. "They had the blood of souls clinging to them; for they had borne a public testimony to the falsehood of the gospel." Their consciences did not rest until they had drawn up a declaration of their faith, had submitted it to the bishop, and had been excommunicated with a few others who had stood firm in their faith. One of these was the priest Haroutioun Baltasarian. Those two priests, Vertanes and Haroutioun, while intimate friends, were in temperament at opposite poles. While the former was the man of action, the latter was rather of a scholarly and meditative turn of mind. Extremely modest and retiring, Haroutioun, contrary to his own conscience and to the repeated intreaties of his missionary friends, had for years been outwardly conforming himself to the usages of the church in the fulfilment of his priestly functions. But the excommunication of Vertanes and the subsequent persecution compelled him to take a determined stand for the truth as he saw it. Stephen had received orders from Constantinople to anathematize and excommunicate all who belonged to the evangelical party in his diocese. Haroutioun, as one of the public suspects in Nicomedia, was among the first to be examined with reference to his religious convictions. Thrice Stephen counseled and warned him. Then he called upon him to write out a confession of his faith which should be publicly read in church in order to clear him of the suspicion of heresy.

Haroutioun, however, not content with a positive declaration of his faith which he drew up according to the bishop's request, addressed to him in addition a letter which set forth in unmistakable terms his position with regard to the teachings of the church. "All her demands," said he, "which accord with the Holy Scriptures, being infallible, I receive. But whatever rival ceremonial demands the church makes, in view of what the apostle threatens, saying, 'If we or an angel from heaven, even, shall preach any other gospel, let him be accursed,' I fear to receive." This letter threw his enemies into a frenzy of rage. On the following Sunday, February 8, Haroutioun was conducted to the church, and Stephen publicly read his statements, and pronounced him excommunicated and anathema. "No more Haroutioun for us! No more Haroutioun!" reiterated the bishop in the hearing of an enraged congregation, while the meek priest, sitting in his corner near the high altar, quietly retorted, "There *is* a Haroutioun;[1] there *is* a Judgment!" Two priests stepped forward and violently tore off Haroutioun's clerical robes, and then the rabble fell upon him and with kicks and blows drove him into the street as a rejected member of the body of Christ. The shearing of his sacerdotal beard completed his disgrace, and imprisonment served to fill up the measure of his penalty. And thus he was compelled to turn his

---

[1] *Haroutioun* means "resurrection." As a proper name it is the equivalent of the Greek Anastasius.

back upon the church he had loved so long and so well. Haroutioun's parishioners declared that they would not have another priest in his place. But to seek to be reinstated in the priesthood was not his purpose. "They plunged me into the waters," he said; "I struggled against the tide; but before I could take a breath, they pushed me in, again and again, till I was drowned. And now I am dead to my former character and position. I obtained a new life in Christ."

For nearly five months from the excommunication of Vertanes, the patriarch's anathemas resounded in the churches of the metropolis. When new names failed him, Matthew reanathematized the old ones. Finally, on June 21, 1846, on the occasion of the festival of Etschmiadzin, he issued a bull of perpetual excommunication and anathema against all Protestants, to be publicly read at every annual return of that festival throughout the churches. And what had occurred in western Europe at the time of the Great Reformation was now repeated on a smaller scale in the Armenian church: the reformers, originally a party within the church, excluded from the church's fellowship and ordinances, found themselves under the necessity of forming a rival organization outside the church.

The members of the Evangelical Union having addressed to the missionaries at Constantinople a written request for counsel and aid in the organization of an independent church, on June 25, 1846, a conference was convened at the capital of all missionaries of the American Board, and a few others competent to the deliberations proposed, and a constitution was drawn up for the Armenian Evangelical Church about to be organized.[1] This constitution provided for a form of government half-way between Congregationalism and Presbyterianism. The officers of the church were to be bishops or pastors, and deacons, chosen by the male members of the local church, and set apart to their office by prayer and the laying on of hands. The disciplinary authority of the local church was to be vested in a church session or standing committee, composed of the deacons and three or more representatives of the people, and presided over by the pastor. The congregation of male members was to have the right of revision in all matters of discipline, and a body composed of the pastors and delegates of the associated churches was to be the final court of appeal. A pastor was to be responsible only to this body. All Christian discipline being spiritual in its nature, anathema and temporal penalty were not to be resorted to under any circumstances.[2] The doctrine of the church

[1] See *Manifesto and Brief Confession of Faith of the Armenian Evangelical Church;* also *Christianity Revived in the East,* pp. 277 ff., and *Missionary Herald,* September, 1846, pp. 317 ff.

[2] This form of government was later somewhat altered. The discipline of the local church was directly vested in the body of its male members, the church session having no more than advisory powers. It was provided that matters of discipline should in case of necessity be appealed to a representative body

was embodied in a confession of faith composed of twelve articles to which all candidates for church membership were publicly to express their assent. This confession, framed in the very heat of the battle between the evangelical and the orthodox ideas of Christian truth, deserves here to be verbally reproduced:

1. Do you believe in the existence of one only living and true God, the creator, preserver, and governor of the universe; omnipotent, omniscient, omnipresent; self-existent, independent, immutable; possessed of infinite benevolence, wisdom, holiness, justice, mercy, and truth, and who is the only proper object of worship?

2. Do you believe that God exists in three persons, the Father, the Son, and the Holy Spirit; and that these three are one God?

3. Do you believe that the Scriptures of the Old and New Testaments were given by inspiration of God, and are a revelation of his will to men, and the sufficient and only rule of faith and practice?

4. Do you believe that mankind, in their natural state, are destitute of holiness, and totally depraved and justly exposed to the wrath of God?

5. Do you believe that the Lord Jesus Christ, perfect God and perfect Man, is the only Savior of sinners, and the only Mediator and Intercessor between God and man; and that by his perfect obedience, sufferings, and death, he made full atonement for sin, so that all who believe in him will assuredly be saved; and that there is no other sacrifice for sin?

6. Do you believe that in consequence of the utter wicked-

of associated churches whose authority should be final; but presbyterial organization and government were left to local discretion. See *Guide for Members of the Evangelical Church*, pp. 33, 45, 54, 57.

ness of man, it is necessary that all should be regenerated by the power of the Holy Spirit, in order to be saved?

7. Do you believe that we are justified by the righteousness of Christ alone, through faith, and not by any fastings, alms, penances, or other deeds of our own; and that while good works are inseparable from a true and living faith, they can never be the meritorious ground of salvation before God?

8. Do you believe that holiness of life, and a conscientious discharge of the various duties we owe to God, to our fellow-men, and to ourselves, are not only constantly binding upon all believers, but essential to the Christian character?

9. Do you believe that, besides God, no other being is to be worshiped and adored, and that all three persons of the sacred Trinity are worthy of our worship, which, to be acceptable, must be offered through no other mediation than that of Jesus Christ the only Mediator; and that the use of relics, crosses, pictures, and images of any sort, in any act of worship, and of the intercession of the saints, is directly opposed to the Scriptures, and highly displeasing to God; and that prayer for the dead is not authorized in the Word of God?

10. Do you believe that there will be a resurrection of the dead, both of the just and of the unjust, and a day of judgment; and that the happiness of the righteous, and the punishment of the wicked, commence at death, and continue forever?

11. Do you believe that any number of true Christians, duly organized, constitute a Church of Christ, of which Christ is the only Head; and that the only sacraments of the church are baptism and communion; baptism being the seal of the covenant, and a sign of the purifying operation of the Holy Spirit, and the token of admission into the visible church; and the communion, in showing forth by visible symbols the death of Christ, being a perpetual memento of his atoning love, and a pledge of union and communion with him and with all true believers?

12. Do you believe that the preaching of the gospel is the great instrument which Christ appointed for the conversion of men and for the edification of his people, and that it is the duty of his church to carry into effect the Savior's command, "Go ye into all the world, and preach the gospel to every creature"?

This constitution was formally adopted by the evangelicals of Constantinople on July 1, 1846. On that day they assembled in the mission chapel at Pera.[1] After Scripture-reading and prayer the constitution was read in their hearing and each article explained. A vote was then taken on the articles of government and discipline, and afterward the evangelicals were called upon to give their assent to the confession of faith, which they did as they rose to their feet, and declared, "We do thus believe." Then, a form of covenant having been assented to, the missionaries, Dwight, Goodell, Schauffler, Homes, Hamlin, Wood, and Van Lennap, and other ministers of the gospel who were present by invitation, arose and in behalf of all evangelical churches acknowledged the new organization thus constituted "as a true church of Jesus Christ." The names of the members of this First Armenian Evangelical Church of Constantinople—of whom there were forty, all with three exceptions males—were then enrolled, after which the church proceeded to the election of officers. Absalom Hatschadourian, afterward called Utijian, was elected first pastor of this church.

[1] The mission chapel was in Dwight's hired house, opposite the grounds of the British embassy.

On the basis of the above-described constitution evangelical churches were organized by the missionaries during the months of July and August in Nicomedia, Adabazar, and Trebizond, the churches in the first two places named being composed each of fourteen members, the church in Trebizond of nine. At the end of a year the infant church of Constantinople had more than doubled its membership, and the aggregate membership of the four churches was about one hundred and forty, while the total number of Armenians, including men, women, and children, who had withdrawn from the national church was over one thousand.

After the consummation of their ecclesiastical organization, their civil recognition by the Turkish government was made the important object of endeavor by the evangelicals. A meeting of the "Protestant Nation" was called at Constantinople on August 17, 1846, when an executive committee of four was appointed to represent the community in its "external relations." On June 16, 1847, this committee passed the following resolution: "Resolved, That we submit a petition to our Lord the Padishah requesting our separation from the Armenian community and the granting of a berat [charter] similar to the berats of the other communities." Four petitions on the subject of this resolution were sent in to the Sultan within the space of a few months.

However, but for the mediation of the British embassy, the petitions of the Protestants might have gone unheeded. To Lord Cowley (Hon. H. R. Wellesley), who occupied the post of Sir Stratford Canning, afterward Lord Stratford de Redcliffe, during a temporary visit of the latter in England, belongs the honor of obtaining, on November 15, 1847, the first imperial iradé recognizing the Protestants of Turkey as a separate community and granting them freedom of conscience and worship.[1]

But it was not until the year 1850 that the rights and privileges of the Protestant community were permanently defined by imperial firman and the Protestants were authorized to elect a chancellor or civil head.[2]   Pursuant to a resolution passed on July 31, 1849, the Executive Committee of the Protestant community at Constantinople had sent in a petition to the British ambassador asking him to use his influence to secure the sanction of the Porte for the appointment of a civil head for the Protestant

[1] The English translation of this charter will be found in the *Missionary Herald* for March, 1848, pp. 98 f.; in *Christianity Revived in the East*, pp. 285 f.; and in Prime, *Goodell's Memoirs*, p. 483. It may here be observed that the recognition of a Protestant community in Turkey secured freedom of conscience for Protestants of all races throughout the Ottoman dominions, and not for Armenian Protestants alone.

[2] While Stephen Seropian was by the iradé of 1847 appointed *Vekeel* or Civil Head of the Protestant community, he was actually authorized to serve only under the title of *Kapou Oghlan*, or Agent at the Porte, and the general oversight of the civil affairs of the community was committed to Izzet Pasha, comptroller of the city revenue. The Kapou Oghlan was elected by the community annually.

community. Lord Stratford de Redcliffe, the great champion of religious liberty in Turkey,[1] who was at this time back at his post at Constantinople, accordingly mediated for the Protestants at the Sublime Porte, and on November 27, 1850, secured from Sultan Abdul Medjid an imperial firman, which rendered into English reads as follows:

To my Vizier, Mohammed Pasha, Prefect of the Police at my Capital, the honorable Minister and glorious Counselor, the Model of the World, and Regulator of the Affairs of the Community, who, directing the public interests with sublime prudence, consolidating the structure of the empire with wisdom, and strengthening the columns of its prosperity and

[1] Lord Stratford was involved in 1843–44 in a dispute with the Porte by virtue of which he found himself committed thenceforward to the defense of religious liberty in Turkey. The dispute referred to was over the execution of Joachim, an Armenian young man, for "apostasy" from Islam (Joachim through fear had professed Mohammedanism, and had later returned to his old faith), and it resulted in the British ambassador's securing from the Sultan in a private audience on March 23, 1844, this personal assurance: "Henceforward neither shall Christianity be insulted in my dominions, nor shall Christians be in any way persecuted for their religion." On the strength of this promise, Sir Stratford demanded toleration for the Protestant Armenians in 1846; and it was mainly through his influence that such toleration was gradually secured. The successive steps in the civil emancipation of the evangelicals prior to the promulgation of the iradé of 1847 were marked by the following events: The shops of the boycotted evangelicals of Constantinople are ordered opened (May, 1846); a vizierial letter is secured in behalf of the persecuted evangelicals of Erzroom (July); a warrant for a Protestant burial is issued by the government at the capital (August); the first Protestant marriage is solemnized at Constantinople without the patriarch's voucher (January, 1847).

glory, is the recipient of every grace from the Most High. May God prolong his glory!

When this sublime and august Mandate reaches you, let it be known that,

Whereas, Hitherto those of my Christian subjects who have embraced the Protestant faith, in consequence of their not being under any specially appointed superintendence, and in consequence of the patriarchs and primates of their former sects, which they have renounced, naturally not being able to attend to their affairs, have suffered much inconvenience and distress; and

Whereas, In necessary accordance with my Imperial compassion, which is the support of all, and which is manifested to all classes of my subjects, it is contrary to my Imperial pleasure that any one class of them should be exposed to suffering; and

Whereas, By reason of their faith, the above-mentioned are already a separate community,

Therefore, it is my Royal compassionate will, that, by all means, measures be adopted for facilitating the administration of their affairs, so that they may live in peace, quiet, and security.

Let, then, a respectable and trustworthy person, acceptable to and chosen by themselves, from among their own number, be appointed, with the title of "Agent of the Protestants," who shall be attached to the Prefecture of the Police.

It shall be the duty of the Agent to have under his charge the register of the members of the community, which shall be kept at the police; and the Agent shall cause to be registered therein all births and deaths in the community. And all applications for passports and marriage licenses, and all petitions on affairs concerning the community that are to be presented to the Sublime Porte, or to any other department, must be given in under the official seal of the Agent.

For the execution of my will, this my Imperial Sublime

Mandate and August Command has been especially issued and given from my Sublime Chancery.

Hence, you, the minister above named, according as it has been explained above, will execute to the letter the preceding ordinance; only, as the collection of the capitation tax and the delivery of passports are subject to particular regulations, you will not do anything contrary to those regulations. You will not permit anything to be required of them, on pretense of fees or on other pretenses, for marriage licenses or registration. You will see to it that like the other communities of the empire, in all their affairs, such as the procuring of cemeteries and places of worship, they have every facility and every needed assistance. You will not permit that any of the other communities shall in any way interfere with their edifices, or with their worldly matters or concerns, or, in short, with any of their affairs, either secular or religious, that thus they may be free to exercise the usages of their faith.

And it is enjoined upon you not to allow them to be molested an iota in these particulars, or in any others; and that all attention and perseverance be put in requisition to maintain them in quiet and security. And, in case of necessity, they shall be free to make representations regarding their affairs through their Agent to the Sublime Porte.

When this my Imperial will shall be brought to your knowledge and appreciation, you will have this August Decree registered in the proper department, and then give it over to remain in the hands of these my subjects. And see you to it, that its requirements be always in future performed in their full import.

Thus know you, and respect my sacred signet!

Written in the holy month of Moharrem, year of the Hegira 1267.

Given in the well-guarded city of Constantinople.[1]

---

[1] *Missionary Herald*, April, 1851, pp. 114 f.; Prime, *Goodell's Memoirs*, pp. 483 f.

On his own invitation a delegation of thirteen men from the Protestant community waited on the British ambassador on the day following the issuance of this imperial firman.   Lord Stratford communicated to these men the contents of the decree, and addressed them for three-quarters of an hour, at times with much emotion.   He told them that the eyes of the world were upon them, because they were the first in Turkey to be freed from the bondage of superstition and to know the gospel in its purity, and exhorted them ever to adhere to the ideals of the gospel of Christ, maintaining a high standard of citizenship among themselves and of brotherly deportment toward the other sects of the land.   On December 13, 1850, at a popular meeting of the Protestant community at Constantinople, this firman was publicly read, and Stephen Seropian, a brother to ex-Patriarch Jacob, who since 1847 had been acting as agent at the Porte, was elected civil head of the community.

It is not to be supposed that the imperial decrees of emancipation secured the immediate cessation of all persecution.   Organized persecution was no longer in order when the first of them had been issued. But it is not in the nature of imperial edicts to overcome bigotry, and passion, and prejudice.   Wherever the new sect was first introduced it had to make a place for itself against more or less violent opposition on the part of the people; and for a number of years after the emancipation of the Protestant community, those who professed evangelical sentiments were subject to petty persecutions not only in provinces far removed from the imperial city, but to some extent in that city itself.[1]

An account of the beginnings of Armenian Protestantism would not be complete without at least briefly relating the events which led up to the establishment of Protestantism among the Turkish-speaking Armenians of the region of Aintab. The pioneer in this field was the vartabed Peter Jizmejian, who was won to the Protestant cause through intercourse with evangelicals at Constantinople in 1842. Peter was the very first man to be taken in hand by the crafty Matthew. He had refused to offer the sacrifice of the mass, and had in so doing betrayed his evangelical convictions. Matthew offered him a charge on the Russian frontier, hoping thus to remove him from the capital, and upon Peter's declining the offer urged him to go to the Armenian monastery at Jerusalem. Peter left Constantinople

[1] A notable outburst of popular fanaticism against Protestants occurred in the year 1860 in the Balat quarter of Constantinople, where a mob kept possession of the Armenian cemetery for four days and nights, and ultimately, in the face of government officers and foreign ambassadors, succeeded in preventing the interment of the remains of Garabed Mirikelam, a charter member of the First Evangelical Church of Constantinople, in consecrated ground. Mirikelam's body was buried by Turkish hands in the public highway. But the consequence of this event was that all Protestants throughout the empire were thereafter allowed to have their own burying-grounds, as also the imperial firman had provided ten years before.

in the fall of 1844, but not to go as far as Jerusalem. Divesting himself on the way of his sacerdotal beard and robes, he proceeded to Beirut. Azariah Smith, missionary of the American Board, then in Syria, presently made his acquaintance and offered to employ him as colporteur in the region of Aintab, Killis, and Aleppo. Peter accepted this offer, and did faithful work. He had not been long in the field before he reported a rapid sale of books, and a good degree of religious interest. In the summer of 1846 several of the most prominent men of Aintab signed a letter addressed to the missionaries at Beirut, petitioning in behalf of two hundred families for a regularly appointed missionary to instruct them in the Scriptures; and in January, 1848, the year preceding his death, Peter saw a church of eight members organized in that city.[1] In October of the same year Azariah Smith established there a mission station. In May of the following year Benjamin Schneider

---

[1] Besides Peter, a certain traveling vartabed, Michael by name, labored at Aintab for a short time. Michael appeared in the city in the spring of 1845. He soon came to be regarded as an eloquent preacher and a fearless reformer. On three different occasions he preached to large congregations in the Armenian church of the city against the confessional, the worship of saints, and other like essentials of Armenian orthodoxy; and when the doors of the church were finally closed against him, he preached to large audiences in private houses, and continued the agitation until the local ecclesiastical authorities effected his expulsion from the city. Michael on his journey westward through Asia Minor after a time fell into disrepute among the evangelicals on account of an appetite for intoxicating drink; but his agitation at Aintab had served a good purpose.

of the Brousa station joined him. Then began a period of great missionary activity for the evangelicals of Aintab. Men uneducated but "full of faith and courage" were sent out with their tools in one hand and the Bible in the other to proclaim the gospel in the regions around. Eleven times these lay evangelists were driven out from Marash alone; but they entered the city for the twelfth time and stayed. From Aintab as a center the evangelical movement thus spread to Kessab, Killis, Oorfa, Marash, and Adana. Already in 1850 it could be stated that the number of Protestants in the region of Aintab was as great as in all the rest of the empire, if not actually greater. When in 1861 Dwight visited this field, the church of Aintab had over two hundred and fifty communicants on its roll, more than a thousand attended its weekly services, and a Sunday school of over sixteen hundred men, women, and children had been gathered in by its workers. The Protestant community in Marash compared favorably with that in Aintab.

The ten years following the Protestant emancipation were years of unprecedented growth for the Armenian missions of the American Board. When we look at the statistics given by the board for those missions at the opening of the year 1850, we find that the Armenian work was not then great in its scope. The board at that time reports seven mission stations in the Armenian field—Constantinople, Bebek, Brousa, Smyrna, Trebizond, Erzroom, and Aintab;

six outstations—Nicomedia, Adabazar, Rodosto, Diarbekir, Oorfa, and Cesarea; eighteen missionaries and twenty female assistant missionaries; five native pastors and one native preacher; twenty native teachers and other helpers; eight churches, two of them at Constantinople, with an aggregate membership of about two hundred and forty souls; two seminaries with nearly fifty students of both sexes, and seven free schools with about one hundred and ten pupils. But before the end of the year, came the promulgation of the imperial firman, and the whole country was opened up to missionary operations. The anathemas of Matthew had already served the purpose of heralding in remote corners of the empire the presence of the new doctrines; and the edict of 1850 everywhere awakened a general readiness to listen to the preaching of the Protestants. About one hundred towns and villages around Aintab, Marash, Oorfa, Diarbekir, Arabkir, Agn, Sivas, Cesarea, Tocat, and Marsovan began to give signs of an awakening, and from remote localities came requests to the missionaries for preachers of the gospel. Sahakian wrote in 1852,[1] while on an eight-months' missionary tour in Armenia: "I am not aware that I have yet visited a single place where Armenians are found, where there is not either an

---

[1] Sahakian returned to his native land in 1848, after a five-years' sojourn in the United States where he received his theological education, and was at the time in question pastor of the evangelical church at Adabazar.

actual awakening, or a preparation of mind for the reception of the truth." When the tour had been completed he expressed the opinion that in that same year forty preachers of the gospel were absolutely needed, and that in the following year twice that number would barely meet the needs of the field. The work was pushed forward, and by the year 1860 the field had become so extensive as to necessitate its subdivision into the three separate missions which have since been maintained, namely, the Western Turkey Mission (including what is now the European Turkey Mission), the Central Turkey Mission, and the Eastern Turkey Mission. For these three missions combined the board at the beginning of that year reports as follows: Twenty-three stations;[1] sixty-five outstations; over fifty male missionaries and about as many female assistant missionaries; about one hundred and eighty native teachers, preachers, and other helpers; forty evangelical churches with a total membership of nearly thirteen hundred souls; seven pastors and thirty-three unordained preachers; two higher schools of learning with about ninety students of both sexes, and one hundred free schools with about twenty-eight hun-

[1] These stations were located at the following points: Constantinople, Smyrna, Bardizak, Tocat, Sivas, Cesarea, Yozgat, Marsovan, Adrianople, Philippopolis, and Eski-Zagra, in the Western Turkey Mission; Aintab, Marash, Oorfa, Aleppo, and Antioch, in the Central Turkey Mission; Mosul, Diarbekir, Mardin, Bitlis, Erzroom, Arabkir, and Harpoot, in the Eastern Turkey Mission.

dred pupils, of whom not a small proportion came from orthodox families.[1]

Such was the early progress of Protestantism among the Armenians of Turkey. Matthew, who as patriarch had said, "I will labor until my death for the extermination of Protestantism in my nation," lived to see it all. Faithful also to his declaration, he fought the new heresy to the very last. In 1858 he was elected catholicos of all the Armenians, and escorted with great pomp and ceremony to the supreme patriarchal seat at Etschmiadzin. But he met in Russian Armenia the same pestilential heresy that had ruffled the peace of his mind in Turkey. The mission of the Evangelical Missionary Society of Basel at Shousha, established with imperial sanc-

[1] The figures here given are compiled from the annual surveys of the missions of the American Board in the *Missionary Herald* for January, 1851, pp. 5, 6, and January, 1861, pp. 4–6. Cf. article "Armenia" in Bliss, *Encyclopaedia of Missions* (1891), Vol. I, p. 102. The following figures, based on the latest annual report (1908) of the American Board, will help the reader to form an idea of the present magnitude of the work of the board in the Turkish empire, which is still almost exclusively among the Armenians: stations, 20; outstations, 269; missionaries and wives, 195; ordained preachers, 92; unordained preachers, 102; teachers and other native workers, 852; organized churches, 130; communicants, 15,748; adherents, 41,802; Sunday schools, 306; Sunday-school membership, 34,119; theological schools, 5; students for the ministry, 25; colleges, boarding, and high schools, 49; students in the same, 4,600; other schools, 312; pupils in the same, 16,191; native contributions, $128,273. These figures may also be taken as practically representing the entire Armenian Protestantism of Turkey, as Protestant Armenian interests in the empire not included in them are a negligible quantity.

tion in 1823 by Dittrich and Zaremba, although suppressed by imperial ukase in 1835, had borne its fruit. Sergius Hampartzoumian, a young man of Schamakhi originally enlightened upon a visit of Zaremba's to his native town in 1828, and later educated in the Russian Baltic province of Esthonia among German evangelical friends, had in 1842 established in Schamakhi a school which had become a strong evangelistic agency. Throughout the pontificate of the catholicos Nerses his heresy had spread unchecked. Now it devolved upon Matthew to defend the interests of orthodoxy. On May 7, 1861, Matthew issued a bull of excommunication against the Protestants at Schamakhi, inflicting penalties similar to those following upon his anathemas in Turkey. Subsequently, by an order of the governor of the Caucasus, the Grand Duke Michael, signed January 12, 1865, the evangelical community in Schamakhi, numbering over three hundred men, women, and children, was permitted to attach itself to the Evangelical Lutheran Consistory of Moscow, on condition that it would maintain no relations with the German colonies in Georgia or any missionary bodies abroad. Matthew died in the following September, having just witnessed a second victory of the new sect, which, spreading rapidly in Baku, Tiflis, Shousha, Alexandropol, and Erivan, was one day to build up a strong community in Valarshabad itself, at the very gates of Etschmiadzin.

What were the chief results of the Protestant Reformation in the Armenian church?

First, *the introduction of Protestant teaching among the Armenians in the first half of the last century averted a serious crisis in religious thought.* The destruction of the Janissaries (1826), the abolition of distinctions in costume between Mohammedans and Christians, the institution of quarantines, and the promulgation of the Hatti-Sherif of Gulhané (1839), all occurring within the space of fifteen years, were indicative of a new order of things in Turkey. The influx of western trade and the introduction of new and rapid modes of travel tended also to promote at this time a social and intellectual quickening which heralded a new age. It was significant of great changes in Turkey that the voyage between Smyrna and Constantinople, which at the time of the first arrival of the American missionaries at the capital occupied from a week to a month, was, in 1835, by the establishment of a steamship line between the two cities, reduced to a matter of only forty-eight hours. The age of the Armenian newspaper, too, was at this time beginning to dawn. In 1840—the year following the founding of *The Repository of Useful Knowledge*, published at Smyrna (1839–42, 1844–46) under the auspices of the American mission—appeared Baltasarian's *Daybreak on Ararat* (Smyrna, 1840–86), the precursor of a multitude of periodical publications[1]

---

[1] The first Armenian periodical known to history is a monthly in the classical tongue, the *Herald*, published by the priest

—the *Herald* (1840–41) and the *Advertiser* (1840
–47 ?) of Constantinople, the *Polyhistor* of Venice
(1843–), the *Patriot* of Calcutta (1845–52),
the *Caucasus* of Tiflis (1846–48), the *Armenia* of
Constantinople (1846–52), the *Europe* of Vienna
(1847–63), the *Masis*[1] of Constantinople (1852–),
the *Aurora* of Moscow (1858–64), the *Bee* of Tiflis
(1858–86), and a number of other publications of
more or less note—which, while some of them proved
very short-lived, bore witness to the fact that Armenian journalism had come to stay.   Now it was but
natural that the new life and thought of which these
were a few indications should bring in their train the
questioning of the old creed.   It was plain that the
old faith which had greatly degenerated into superstition could not much longer be preserved in its old
form.   A more rational understanding of Christian
truth must be inculcated.   In the absence of this,
French materialism and infidelity were sure to lay
hold upon awakened minds.   This one service,
therefore, among others, Protestantism rendered
the Armenian people: it placed an alternative
before them for infidelity, so repugnant to the
average Armenian mind, and made it possible for

Haroutioun Schmavonian, at Madras, India, 1794–96.   The next
in order deserving the name is the *Byzantine Telescope*, a bi-
weekly journal published at Venice, 1812–16.

[1] In 1879 *Masis* became a daily—the first published in the
Armenian tongue, with the exception of the *Mschak* of Tiflis
(founded in 1872) which began to appear daily in the preceding
year—and continued as such until 1884.

them to preserve the old faith, while discarding the old form.

In the next place should be mentioned *the benefit which the Armenian church derived from the evangelical movement in its emancipation from the influence of Rome.* We have already seen in another chapter to what extent the influence of Latin thought was felt in the Armenian church in the early decades of the last century. We might here add that Tschamourjian, the great champion of the church's orthodoxy, and the patriarch Matthew, the great persecutor of the Protestants, themselves had a tinge of Romanism in their thought. Matthew's emphasis in his "New Creed" on the sacrament of extreme unction and the infallibility of the church was inspired more by Roman teaching than by Armenian. Now the reformers made it always a special object to point out to the orthodox Armenians that, in some things, at least, the Armenian church was as far removed from Romanism as the Protestants themselves were; and if Armenian writers of the latter half of the last century, and Matthew among others, are as pronounced in their denunciation of Romanism as they are in their condemnation of Protestantism, they received their first lessons from the Protestants. The debt of gratitude which the Armenian church owed the evangelical movement in this regard was so well recognized, that old-school Armenians repeatedly confessed, even in the earlier years of that movement, that Protestant thought had saved the Armenian church from the power of the papal propaganda.

As a third result of the evangelical movement we may mention *the establishment, for the first time, of a civil-ecclesiastical community in Turkey that maintained in practice the strict separation of church and state, and thus insured freedom of conscience to all its membership.* In the old communities in Turkey there was no distinction made between church and state. Every member of a civil community was *de facto* also a member of the church which gave its name to the community. The patriarch was himself the personal embodiment of this union of church and state: he was both an ecclesiastical officer and a civil magistrate. Everyone under this system who renounced his church thereby also renounced the civil body of which he was a member, made himself an outlaw in the eyes of the Turkish government, and risked the persecuting wrath of his patriarch. The Protestant community was established on a different basis. There the line of demarkation between church and state was very strictly observed. The civil representative of the Protestant community was a layman possessed of no ecclesiastical authority; while by virute of the Protestant system of church-membership which recognizes only those who have made a satisfactory profession of their faith before the local churches, a person who claimed membership in the Protestant civil community was not necessarily a member of the Protestant ecclesiastical organization. From this resulted a type of religious liberty unknown before in the Turkish empire. A man might belong to any one of a number of different Protestant sects, or might belong to none; yet as a member of the Protestant civil community he was entitled to the care of the Protestant Chancery and to the protection of the Ottoman government.

Above all and as inclusive of all the results of the evangelical movement should be mentioned *the spiritual religion which was its peculiar boon to the Armenian people and to oriental Christendom*. It may be difficult to say whether emphasis should have been placed more on the educational or on the evangelistic method of missionary work among the oriental churches in the early years of the American missions in the Levant. But this one thing is certain that the evangelistic method at this time enforced a lesson which no other method exclusively employed could have served to enforce, namely, that God is a Spirit, and they that worship him must worship him in spirit and in truth. The lack of spirituality in the Armenian church is nowhere more in evidence —outside of its public worship—than in its lifeless doctrine of faith. The Armenian church, in common with the other Eastern churches, has too often overlooked the vital character of Christian faith. The first article of the "New Creed" of the patriarch Matthew betrays the misconception under which those churches have for so long labored. Faith to them has been synonymous, and only synonymous, with creed. And with that conception of Christian faith it is small wonder that Matthew finds no essential relation between faith and works, nor a sufficient ground in faith for human salvation. For the first time in many centuries Protestant preaching taught the churches of the East in general and the Armenian church in particular the all-important truth that faith is not a thing of the lips, but a principle of the life; and, removing the conception of faith from the sphere of the purely intellectual and human, declared faith to be of the essence of an inner relationship to God in Christ, a vital principle, and as such the all-sufficient ground of salvation before God.

This chapter should not be brought to a close without a special notice of the missionary Dwight, the "father of the Armenian mission."

Harrison Gray Otis Dwight was born at Conway, Mass., in the year 1803. His parents removed not long after his birth to Utica in the state of New York, where at the age of fifteen he was converted in a revival and became a communicant in the Third Presbyterian Church. He was graduated at Hamilton College in 1825, and at Andover Theological Seminary three years later. While in the latter institution he offered himself to the American Board and was assigned to the mission of the Levant. He was ordained at Great Barrington, Mass., in 1829, and sailed from Boston on January 21, 1830. He arrived at Malta on the 27th of the following month. The researches of Smith and Dwight in Armenia were undertaken in March, 1830, and occupied somewhat more than a year. At the end of that time the missionary explorers returned to Malta, and Dwight there received instructions to join Goodell at Constantinople. He arrived at Constantinople June 5, 1832; and from that time onward for almost thirty years the Turkish capital was the scene of his labors. He was killed in a railroad accident at Shaftesbury, Vermont, January 25, 1862.

The uniformity of Dwight's life as a missionary was broken by few incidents. Except when some short exploring tour, or a visit to some town otherwise destitute of missionary influence, or an occasional visit to his own native land, called him away for a time, he was steadily employed at Constantinople teaching, and preaching, and expounding the Scriptures. And therein lies the significance of his life with reference to the evangelical movement. For thirty years he was the foremost religious instructor and guide of the inner circle of Armenian evangelicals; and thus he became what Sahakian termed him, "the chief founder of the Apostolic and Evangelical Church of Armenia."

By the time those thirty years were numbered Dwight's eyes seemed to see "the salvation of the Lord." In January, 1861, eight months before his final return to his native land, he undertook a tour of inspection over the entire field which the missions of the American Board then occupied in Turkey, and more than once he expressed his readiness to say like Simeon of old, "Now lettest thou thy servant depart in peace." There was a keen sense of satisfaction in his words:

I have now completed my work. I have visited every station of the Board actually occupied, in the Turkish and Persian empires, excepting those among the Bulgarians. It has been my privilege to see all the missionaries and their families,—a rare body of men and women, of whom our churches and our country may well be proud,—and also to become personally acquainted with hundreds and thousands of the dear Protestant brethren and sisters of this land— God's lights in the midst of surrounding darkness, God's witnesses where the very seat of Satan is.

CHAPTER VIII

WHY A PROTESTANT ARMENIAN CHURCH?

The missions of the American Board to the oriental churches, more specifically the missions to the Armenian church, were originally committed to a policy of strict non-proselytism—a policy which had for its sole aim the instilling into those churches of evangelical ideas and ideals without alienating any of their members from them. The "instructions" of the Prudential Committee of the board to Cyrus Hamlin, delivered on the eve of his departure for the Levant in 1838, dealing with the subject of the oriental churches, declared emphatically: "Our object is not to subvert them; not to pull down, and build up anew. It is to reform them; to revive among them . . . . the knowledge and spirit of the gospel."[1]

The considerations which conspired to commend such a policy were various. In the first place the American Board was originally to a certain degree a non-sectarian organization: it represented not

[1] *Missionary Herald*, January, 1839, p. 41. Goodell virtually acknowledged his action in receiving Bishop Dionysius and the vartabed Gregory into the mission church at Beirut in 1827 as a mistake of his early years of inexperience, when in 1835 he wrote: "When I first came into these countries, I laid hold of individuals, and endeavored to pull them out of the fire; but my aim is now to take hold of whole communities, and, as far as possible, to raise them all up to 'sit together in heavenly places in Christ Jesus.'" See Prime, *Goodell's Memoirs*, p. 179.

only New England Congregationalism, but also the Presbyterian and the Dutch and Associate Reformed churches. Further, any appearance of proselytism was sure to awaken the authorities of the oriental churches to challenge the missionaries' right of residence in Turkey and thus to imperil the missions of the board in the empire; for, while only in the year preceding the arrival of Goodell at Constantinople a treaty of friendship had been concluded between the United States and the Porte, it was generally understood to be strictly commercial in its nature and provisions.[1] Again, by pursuing a proselyting policy the missionaries would run the risk of losing the support of an enlightened element in the native community, who, while desirous of a reformation in the church, would not countenance secession under any circumstances.[2] Finally, it was held that a campaign of evangelism without proselytism promised success in the case of the oriental churches as it did not in the case of the Church of

[1] It was not Mr. Porter alone who held that American missionaries had as such no treaty rights in Turkey (see above, p. 102, note). Goodell himself long labored under the conviction that the missionaries had no right, under the existing treaty, to ask their legation to secure the protection of the Turkish government for their schools. See Prime, *Goodell's Memoirs*, pp. 176 f. Perhaps, however, he was largely influenced in his views on this subject by Mr. Porter's own position.

[2] As an actual fact several friends of the reform party deserted when they discovered that the missionaries and their board were weighing the possibilities of secession. See Dwight, *Christianity Revived in the East*, pp. 127 f.

Rome. To the formation of this conviction the English missionary societies which preceded the American Board in the lands of the East largely contributed. On the testimony of these societies, while the Church of Rome, intrenched behind a doctrine of the supreme authority of the Pope in matters of faith and practice, afforded as a church no avenue of approach to Protestant evangelism, the oriental churches, holding, tacitly at least, to the final authority of the Bible, were essentially evangelical in character and easily accessible to the Protestant missionary, and possessed in themselves a sufficient basis of internal reform. And the pioneer missionaries of the American Board in the Levant readily fell in with this view. Eli Smith, writing from Malta early in 1830, spoke of the opposition met with by the mission in the Levant at the hands of the Church of Rome, and then added:

The spirit of the other churches is essentially different, and we are determined not to call them forth into opposition by a proselyting and controversial course. Our object is not to pull down or build up a sect, but to make known and inculcate the great fundamental truths of the gospel.[1]

In the pursuit of this policy the American missionaries at Constantinople at the first avoided all controversy, improved every opportunity to convey the impression to the native Christians that they were not in Turkey with any sectarian objects at heart, and bent their energies to the task of publication and

[1] *Missionary Herald,* June, 1830, p. 177.

education. Goodell came to Constantinople with a supply of Testaments and tracts of a non-controversial character. On his arrival he sought to secure the adoption of improved methods of primary instruction in the common schools of the city, advocating, and introducing into many of the schools the then modern and improved system which went by the name of Lancasterian. In the fall of 1834 a mission high school was opened at Pera—the first institution of higher learning among the Armenians of Constantinople—and presently the first impulses were given by the American missionaries to female education among the Armenians of the Turkish capital. These early efforts were all based on the theory that what the oriental churches needed above all things else was not more sectarian controversy, but more enlightenment of the kind calculated to arouse a widespread interest in the Word of God.

We have seen, however, that fifteen years from the founding of the Armenian mission the missionaries of the American Board in Turkey were compelled, contrary to their original plan, to establish an independent evangelical church.

There was an immediate cause for this, but we must not seek it, as is sometimes done, in the *persecution* of 1846. The year 1846 was the year of the greatest persecution of the evangelicals, but not the only year of their persecution: the evangelicals suffered their first official persecution in 1839; they endured much petty persecution also from 1841 onward. Further, it should be noted that all official persecution in 1846 had ceased before the first of the evangelical churches was organized. The immediate cause for the organization of the evangelical church in Turkey lay in the excision, final and irrevocable, of the evangelicals.

But it is not to be supposed that the founding of Protestantism in Turkey as a separate sect was the result of a sudden emergency. It is but a partial view of the matter which lays the entire responsibility for the organization of the Armenian Evangelical Church at the door of the patriarch Matthew and his advisers. While the excision of the Protestants served as the immediate cause and public justification of the founding of the Protestant Armenian church, it was not the ultimate cause of it. Back of the immediate cause for schism lay ultimate causes —causes which led the missionaries to look forward to the establishment of a Protestant church in Turkey for some years previous to 1846, and to regard a strict adherence to their original policy of non-proselytism as impracticable.

What were the causes which conspired to discourage the missionaries' adherence to their original policy of non-proselytism, and to effect its final abandonment? Four causes may be given.

1. *The pressure of a popular demand in the home churches for tangible results.*—What we may know on this phase of our subject is to be learned only by "reading between the lines" of the published

correspondence of the mission in the Levant. But probably we shall not far miss the mark if we say that the pressure of popular impatience at home (and the home churches were more impatient in the early days of modern missionary endeavor than at the present time) to a certain extent influenced the missionaries to abandon the more obscure and intangible work of quietly enlightening the oriental churches, and to adopt a method and policy which promised results more easily to be tabulated.

2. *The intolerance of the oriental churches.*—In the summer of 1838 Dwight, having visited Nicomedia in the preceding May, expressed it as his sincere wish that the "brethren" in that city might not secede but might continue in the national church.[1] In November, 1839, he spoke of individuals forsaking their church on account of a change in religious opinion, and of the consequent desirability of the recognition of an evangelical civil community in Turkey, and gave utterance to these significant words: "A separation ought not to be forced, although it will, without doubt, ultimately take place; for light and darkness cannot always exist together."[2] What caused this change of view in such a short space of time? The answer is easily discovered. Dwight had witnessed the persecution of 1839, and had become convinced that the church would not tolerate evangelicalism within her pale. And this being the

[1] *Missionary Herald*, December, 1838, p. 462.

[2] *Ibid.*, September, 1840, p. 355.

case, schism was only a matter of time. That the excision of the evangelicals by the oriental churches, and the consequent necessity of organizing them into a separate church, were generally anticipated by the year 1842, is evident from the following extract of a committee report submitted to and adopted by the American Board at its thirty-third annual meeting at Norwich, Conn., in the September of that year:

Whenever those oriental churches, having had the gospel fairly proposed to them, shall reject it, exscinding and casting out from their communion those who receive it—as the Jewish church exscinded and expelled the primitive believers, and as the Romish church exscinded and expelled the Reformers— then it will be necessary for our missionary brethren to turn from them as apostate, to shake off the dust of their feet as a testimony against them, and to call on all God's children to come out from among them and not to be partakers of their plagues.[1]

3. Closely allied to the intolerance of the church, and underlying it, was *the essential antagonism between oriental orthodoxy and the missionaries' doctrines and methods*, which we may name as another cause of the abandonment of the original policy of non-proselytism.

To begin with, the Armenian church, as it came into contact with the evangelism of the American missionaries, more and more evinced a spirit which was far from the essentially evangelical character originally attributed to the oriental churches. Protestant evangelism was not so congenial to the Arme-

[1] *Missionary Herald*, November, 1842, p. 432.

nian church as had been supposed. The Armenian church, with the other oriental churches indeed, theoretically held to the supreme authority of the Scriptures. But, with the other churches also, it had given place to a great mass of patristic interpretations and ceremonial regulations prescribed by church councils, which had come to be regarded with a veneration next only to that accorded the sacred Scriptures, with the result that the Word of God had been all but lost in the traditions of men.

On the other hand, the missionaries' ideas and methods of evangelism were far too radical for the oriental churches, and certain on that account sooner or later to invite opposition. The missionaries' ideas were of the ultra-evangelical type. Rufus Anderson, the distinguished secretary of the American Board, was voicing the sentiments of the missionaries in the Levant when in 1842 he laid down the principle that the modern missionary should be more radical in his teaching than Luther; that he should insist on discarding all that was not expressly required by the Bible, instead of, like Luther, retaining all that was not expressly forbidden by the Bible. Perhaps it was teaching based on this principle that in the early years of the evangelical movement (1837) prompted an "enlightened" merchant, who went to the patriarchate to take out his marriage license, to refuse to pay the customary fees because their payment was not required in Scripture. As to the missionaries' methods of evangelism, these were radically "evangelistic." At a conference of the mission of the Levant, held at Smyrna, September 27, 1837, it was resolved:

That we regard the public and formal preaching of the gospel as an exceedingly important means for the conversion of men in these countries, as well as in our own, to be employed wherever and whenever Providence opens the way; and that we believe it to be practicable at most of our stations[1]—

an opinion which was readily adopted and urged upon the missionaries of the various stations of the mission by the Prudential Committee of the board. Now the native Christians regarded public preaching as the peculiar function of the church. When, therefore, they saw the missionaries resort to preaching, especially to preaching in order to conversion, they concluded that these men had come, not to spread education, but to establish some sect of their own, and proceeded to treat them like any other intruders. Dwight little understood at the time the "thoughtful and peculiar expression of countenance" with which in the course of an interview in 1835 the Armenian patriarch's vicar turned to him and said: "You will, by and by, become a preacher to the Armenians." In his account of the incident the missionary adds naïvely, "I hope the prophecy will prove true." But we may venture to think that he did understand the vicar's "thoughtful and peculiar expression of countenance" at last when, the latter's prophecy

[1] *Missionary Herald*, April, 1838, p. 116.

proving true in the following year,[1] some of the warmest friends of the reform movement became disaffected, because they saw in the public services of the mission at Constantinople the nucleus of a new sect,[2] and the authorities of the church began to resist the missionaries' efforts at every turn.

By virtue of the mutual reaction of the prelatical traditionalism of the church on the one hand, and the puritanical evangelism of the missionaries on the other, the evangelical Armenians found themselves seceding long before they were excommunicated by patriarchal anathema. Attendance on the sacrifice of the mass early became the great question of conscience in the ecclesiastical life of the evangelicals. While it is clear that different missionaries differed in their counsels to them on this point, the common conscience of the great body of them condemned it as a species of idolatry, and

---

[1] Dwight's first Armenian sermon was preached September 9, 1836.

[2] "October 7, 1842: Today I gave notice of the suspension of our Armenian service for the present. This step was taken to conciliate some of our former friends who have become disaffected, and are strongly opposed to this service, regarding it as the nucleus of a new and separate church organization. Only two individuals, formerly reckoned among the brethren, have as yet taken this stand; though several others feel very decidedly that the meetings ought for a time to be suspended. In deference to their judgment, and in consideration of their exposure, if a storm should arise, we have concluded to omit them for the present."—Dwight's Journal, *Missionary Herald*, July, 1843, p. 273.

many of them preferred to partake of the communion at the "mission church" with the missionaries and their families, rather than in the national churches. And so early as the beginning of 1835 some of them were urging the missionaries to secure the organization of an independent evangelical church, and soon after, the recognition of a Protestant civil community which should insure to them liberty of conscience and make it possible for their numbers greatly to increase. The fact of the whole matter was that as soon as they had embraced the missionaries' views of religion, they found the old church uncongenial. Thus years before the excision of the evangelicals Dwight perceived that evangelical principles and practice, and orthodox principles and practice, were like light and darkness mutually exclusive.

4. *The official recognition of the treaty rights of American missionaries in Turkey by the United States government.*—In response to a memorial of the American missionaries in the Turkish empire submitted to the United States government through ex-Governor Armstrong of Massachusetts, Secretary of State Daniel Webster sent to the United States minister at Constantinople, David Porter, under date of February 2, 1842, a dispatch containing the following words:

It has been represented to this Department that the American missionaries, and other citizens of the United States not engaged in commercial pursuits, residing and travelling in the Ottoman dominions, do not receive from your legation that aid and protection to which, as citizens of the United States, they feel themselves entitled; and I have been directed by the President, who is profoundly interested in the matter, to call your immediate attention to the subject, and to instruct you to omit no occasion, where your inter-. ference in behalf of such persons may become necessary or useful, to extend to them all proper succor and attentions of which they may stand in need, in the same manner that you would to other citizens of the United States who, as merchants, visit or dwell in Turkey.

The strange position which Mr. Porter had assumed with reference to the American missionaries in Turkey—namely, that they were entitled by treaty to the protection of the government of the United States only so long as they refrained from proselyting—was virtually pronounced untenable by this dispatch. No such distinction could be drawn in practice as between proselyting missionaries and non-proselyting missionaries, and it was now to be understood that, if a missionary had any right to reside in the Turkish dominions at all, he was as much entitled, as a citizen of the United States, to the protection of his government *in the pursuit of his calling* as an American merchant was in the pursuit of his. This dispatch from Washington had a very direct bearing on the missionary activities of the American missionaries in Turkey. From 1842 onward they were characterized by greater boldness and aggressiveness than ever before; and, so far as a policy of non-proselytism had been a matter of expediency, it was then flung to the winds.

By these various causes the American missionaries
in the Turkish empire were led to relinquish their
original policy of non-proselytism a number of years
before the final disruption of 1846. Then in place
of it was adopted the policy of only refraining from
taking the initiative in any open rupture with the
mother church. On this revised policy converts
were to be made to Protestantism, but an independent Protestant church was not to be organized until
the evangelical party was forced to it by hierarchi-
cal excision and anathema. That the missionaries
for several years before the Protestant excision
earnestly desired the hastening of the day when
such a church should be established, is clear
from the fact that they made it the subject of special
prayer.

It should here be recorded that the original aim
of enlightening and internally reforming the oriental
churches has never, even since the Protestant excision, been completely abandoned by the American
Board, and that the policy of the board's Turkish
missions has of late years especially reverted to that
original aim. The gaining of converts from those
churches is not indeed in our day deprecated, but it
is not made the sole, or even chief, end of missionary
activity among the Christian races of the Turkish
empire. And it may be affirmed that the promotion
of the counter-reformation still in progress in the
Armenian church is regarded as fully as important
an end in itself as the maintenance of a large Protes-

tant community of 16,000 communicants and 42,000 adherents.[1]

[1] "The strength of our work in Turkey is not measured by the number and size of native evangelical churches, or by the large company who have separated themselves from the old churches and now bear the name Protestant. It is well known that it was never the purpose of the Board or its missionaries to separate a Protestant body from the oriental churches. The separation that did take place in 1846 was due to the action of the ecclesiastics of the old church and not to the missionaries. In all parts of the empire today the process of separation is decreasing, while the old church, both Gregorian and Greek, is shot through and through with thoroughly evangelical ideas and beliefs. Protestant and Gregorian children, side by side in the same schools, study the life of Jesus Christ and listen to the same Christian instruction. The name 'Protestant' is no longer regarded as opprobrious, and the old churches are teaching in many forms the same Christian truths that our missionaries teach. This fact is dwelt upon that no one may think the work has diminished because no reports are made of large accessions to the churches. There have been sweeping revivals, like those at Marash and Harpoot, but even the import of these is not measured by the number who become Protestants, but by the opportunities that are thus created for planting evangelical truth within the precincts of the old church."—"Annual Survey of the Work of the American Board," *Missionary Herald*, November, 1906, p. 545.

CHAPTER IX

THE STRUGGLE FOR DEMOCRACY

There was perhaps nothing more significant of the diffusion of modern ideas among the Armenians of Turkey during the last century than their awakening to the evils of the civil-ecclesiastical system under which they lived. Before the middle of that century there sprang up a popular movement among the Armenians of Constantinople which within twenty years resulted in the complete overthrow of despotism in the Armenian community of Turkey, and the establishment of a constitutional form of government.

Essentially opposed to the rights of the Turkish Armenian populace was the patriarchal system under which they lived. This system, established in the fifteenth century, made the Armenian patriarch of Constantinople, within certain limits, absolute ruler in his own community. And it was capable of much corruption. The patriarchal office, in theory under the control jointly of the clergy of the capital, the magnates, and the clerks of the guilds, was in actual practice often put up at auction by the Turkish government, and given to the highest bidder, with the result that unscrupulous men often came to power who exploited the people until superseded by others more resourceful than themselves.[1]

[1] See *Researches of Smith and Dwight*, Vol. I, pp. 53 ff.

But it was not with the patriarchate directly that the people in the last century joined issue. The patriarchate itself had come to be the toy of a moneyed aristocracy who bought the office for favorites whom they expected to do their bidding, and controlled the affairs of the community to advance their own selfish interests. To fight these aristocratic usurpers involved much less risk than to fight the patriarch himself who was an officer of government, and rebellion against whose authority would have been treated by the Porte as nothing short of rebellion against the Ottoman government. And it promised as much of solid results in the end. The struggle which we are about to review, therefore, was a struggle of democracy against oligarchy, rather than of democracy against monarchy.

The origin of the Armenian moneyed aristocracy is to be traced to the time of Mohammed the Conqueror, by virtue of whose favor a number of influential Armenians rose to positions of power in court and government circles, and thus came to be powerful in their own community also. The name *amira* which was applied to members of this aristocracy, however—a term derived from the Arabic *emir*, meaning ruler or magnate—did not come into common use until after the middle of the eighteenth century. About the year 1840, the time of their greatest numerical strength, the Armenian magnates numbered about two hundred.

These dignitaries were at this time themselves

divided into two warring factions. On the one side were arrayed the *sarrafs*, or magnates of commerce and finance, who wielded immense power in government affairs, by virtue of their connection with provincial pashas and other officials of the Porte who were dependent on them for the necessary purchase and bribery money for office, and for the surety required by the central government for the proper transmission of revenues to the imperial treasury. On the other side were what might be termed the salaried magnates—much fewer in numbers than the others—whose influence at the Porte was that of office rather than that of wealth. Among these were the imperial architects, the superintendents of the imperial powder works, the superintendents of the imperial mint, and the chief baker to the Sultan. The bone of contention was the National College of Scutari.

On the initiative of the imperial architects, Balian and Serverian, and with the co-operation of the tradesmen, the National College was founded and opened in the December of 1838, during Stephen's patriarchate. Youths of promise to the number of fifty at that time were promoted to that institution of learning from the various parochial schools of the capital, to form the first-year class, and the curriculum having been mapped out for four years, accommodations were provided for one hundred and fifty more, to be admitted in classes of fifty each in the course of the following three years. The

Armenian patriarchate of Jerusalem promised the annual sum of 120,000 piastres toward the support of the college.

With the death of Mahmoud, however, in the summer of 1839, the power of the imperial architects waned, and their jealous rivals among the sarrafs, Misakian and Papazian, found the time opportune to upset their educational projects. These sarrafs influenced the patriarch of Jerusalem to withdraw his support, and caused the paying scholars to be removed from the college. Jacob, the patriarch at the capital, tried different plans to save this the only native school of higher learning among the Armenians of Constantinople. At one time a tax of five piastres was levied on every applicant for a traveling passport. At another, subscription papers were circulated in the capital by the parish priests. But all without avail. By the beginning of 1840 it was seen that the college must either be closed or be placed in new hands.

Jacob turned to the people for help. In the March of 1840 he established a central board of finance composed of twenty-four tradesmen to manage the finances of the community, and bring them out of the chaotic state into which they had fallen. The tradesmen, who were shopkeepers and skilled laborers of various descriptions, composed the most important part of the middle class which also numbered in its ranks the lower clergy and parish teachers and government employees of the capital. This

middle class consisted mainly of natives of Constantinople, Smyrna, Banderma, Cesarea, and Divrik.
It was the patriarch's plan that six sarrafs should
co-operate with the twenty-four in the management
of the community's business.

But the sarrafs who as private individuals had so
far antagonized the college of the architects did not
propose to lend it a hand as members of a board.
They refused to sit in council with the tradesmen.
And the result was as they had intended. The
tradesmen, themselves unable to raise the 80,000
piastres in immediate demand, were compelled to
resign.

The appointment of the twenty-four, however,
served a good purpose. The common people were
thereby drawn into the conflict. From now on it
was to be a battle not between two classes of magnates
but between the magnates and the common people.
The patriarch Stephen, the creature of the sarrafs,
had not long been restored to power before the
people began to bestir themselves.

One recent event greatly helped the popular cause.
That was the promulgation, on November 3, 1839,
of the Hatti-Sherif of Gulhané, which delivered a
blow to the powers of the sarrafs from which they
never recovered. For some of these magnates were
financially ruined by this event, and their influence
at the Porte was accordingly destroyed, while others,
who suffered comparatively little financial loss, suffered materially in prestige as their powers for

intrigue were curtailed by the establishment of the right of public trial for every accused party, and their control of the offices of state was curbed with the prohibition of bribery and court favoritism, the provision for stated salaries for all government officials, and the establishment of a regular system of taxation which rendered their surety unnecessary.[1] The articles of the Hatti-Sherif bearing on the points of public taxation, justice, and appointments are the following:

It is of the highest importance to regulate the imposition of the taxes, as the state, which in the defense of its territory is forced into various expenses, cannot procure the money necessary for the army and other branches of the service, save by contributions levied on its subjects.

Although, thanks to God, our subjects have been for some time delivered from the scourge of monopolies, falsely regarded hitherto as a source of revenue, a fatal practice still exists, although it can only have the most disastrous consequences: it is that of the venal concessions known by the name of *iltizim*.

Under this system, the civil and financial administration of a province is intrusted to the arbitrary will of an individual, that is, at times, to the iron hand of the most violent and covetous passions; for, if the administrator is not good, he cares for nothing but his own advantage.

It is therefore necessary that, in future, each member of

[1] That the Hatti-Sherif by no means at one stroke annihilated the influence of the sarrafs at the Porte may be inferred from the fact that in 1842 the government committed to a number of them the collection of the taxes throughout the empire, for which purpose they organized two giant corporations, the one operating in Asiatic, the other in European Turkey.

the Ottoman society should be taxed in a ratio to his fortune and his ability, and that nothing further should be demanded from him.

.   .   .   .

In future, the cause of every accused party will be tried publicly, in conformity with our divine law; and until a regular sentence has been pronounced, no one can put another to death, secretly or publicly, by poison, or any other form of punishment.

.   .   .   .

As all the functionaries of the empire will receive from this day a suitable salary, and those whose functions are not at present sufficiently rewarded will be advanced, a rigorous law will be passed against the traffic in favors and appointments, which the divine laws reprove, and which is one of the principal causes of the decay of the empire.

The conflict came to a head in the spring of 1841. On April 25 of that year a gathering of about three hundred tradesmen in attendance at the closing exercises of the college, after listening to an earnest appeal from the principal, passed a resolution to take the management of the institution into their own hands, and formed themselves into an association for that purpose. The sarrafs had refused to co-operate with the tradesmen. The latter were now determined to assume sole control of the community's affairs.

At the instigation of the sarrafs, the patriarch immediately summoned and rebuked the leaders of this movement. But the tradesmen were not to be daunted, and on the following Friday, April 30, one of their number, accompanied by sixteen of the students of the college, presented the Sultan with a petition. The result was not satisfactory. On July 13 the Porte nominally reinstated the twenty-four tradesmen in their office, but the imperial firman required to confirm their appointment was not issued. On August 26 a popular delegation to the number of about two hundred submitted another petition to the Sultan. This brought only more trouble upon the people. The grand vizier, Rifat Pasha, under orders from his sovereign, summoned the twenty-four and demanded the names of those who had been causing this commotion in the community, and upon their pleading ignorance in the matter, cast them into prison. Learning of this, on September 5, a crowd of two or three thousand men proceeded in a body to the grand vizier's palace. "If you imprison them, imprison us also," they said to the prime minister; "whatever they are guilty of, we are guilty of." Rifat Pasha thought it wise to defer to the will of the people. The twenty-four were released, and the mob dispersed under assurances of the Sultan's interest in their well-being. But toward the end of the month, seven of the leaders of this demonstration—the principal of the college, two priests, and four tradesmen—were quietly sent into exile.

In view of this agitation Stephen was dethroned, and, as a compromise, on October 1, Theodore, a disagreeable old man in his dotage, for whom neither sarrafs nor tradesmen had any respect, was raised to the patriarchal office. In the middle of the same month the college was closed by government orders as an occasion of strife. But neither the change of a patriarch nor the closing of a college could any longer insure peace in the Armenian community. In the latter part of November the tradesmen sent in a petition to the government complaining of the abuses of the sarrafs and stating that while they, the petitioners, were loyal subjects of the Porte, they refused to be ruled by a few magnates. Ambassadors of foreign powers, to whom also petitions had been sent for interference, in the meantime interceded at the Porte in their behalf. At last in the following month the Porte issued peremptory orders to the sarrafs to arrive at some understanding with the tradesmen. Thereupon a popular council of twenty-seven tradesmen, in place of the twenty-four, was elected by the tradesmen to take charge of the community's affairs, and confirmed in office by an imperial edict which insured it both permanency and freedom from aristocratic interference. At the same time the signatures of the patriarch and sarrafs were secured to a charter forever renouncing all jurisdiction in matters pertaining to the domain of the council (December 24, 1841). In the February of the following year the exiles were recalled.

But this triumph of the people was of short duration. The business of the community had not been long in their hands before they discovered that one may defeat an enemy and still fail to hold his domains. They had the determination to manage their own

affairs, but not the competent men to whom the
task could be intrusted or the constitutional powers
to make a popular administration effective.   The
twenty-seven were inexperienced in fiscal matters,
and, to add to the difficulty of the situation, there
was no law by which the wealthy magnates of the
community could be compelled to contribute their
rightful share toward its expenses. Complaints
soon began to irritate the new administration, and
for the second time the representatives of the people
offered to resign their position.

The twenty-seven went to Papazian, at this time
head of the fraternity of sarrafs, and offered to surrender the charter of rights which had been secured
with so great difficulty.   Papazian's politic advice
to them was that they should proceed to the Sublime
Porte and make their statement to the Turkish
government.   So to the Porte they went; declared
before the Supreme Court their incompetency to
manage the affairs of their community, and laid down
the imperial firman which had made them the administrative body of the Armenian nation.   By order of
the Sublime Porte a council was convened at the
patriarchate, the charter of rights bearing the signatures of patriarch and sarrafs was torn up, and
the administration of the community's affairs was
once more turned over to the aristocracy (November 25, 1842).

But the aristocracy was not to assume entire control of affairs permanently.   The sentiment of the

people would not tolerate that.   The conflict between
the magnates and the people had subsided when
Matthew succeeded to the patriarchal throne (July
29, 1844); and being a man who enjoyed popularity
on all hands he was able to secure a compromise
between the hostile factions.   Thus soon after his
accession a council of thirty was appointed, composed of sarrafs and tradesmen in about equal
numbers, to share with him the administrative
authority of the community.   Through his efforts,
too, the college at Scutari, which had been converted
by the government into a military hospital, was
restored to the community and reopened in the
October of 1846.

But Matthew was not long able to maintain har-
monious relations with both factions alike.   The
sarrafs interfered with the patriarch's spiritual
jurisdiction and compelled him to take up a defiant
attitude toward them and to play the rôle of champion
of popular rights.   The result was that the powers of
the aristocracy suffered a new and permanent delim-
itation.   The controversy consisted in the sarrafs'
claiming, and the patriarch's denying them, the
right to a voice in the appointment of the diocesan
bishops.   Matthew insisted that while he felt himself free to consult the sarrafs on matters pertaining
to the civil and fiscal affairs of the community, it
belonged to the people and himself alone to designate
bishops for the provinces.   The sarrafs appealed to
the Porte, complaining that Matthew was managing

the community's affairs without consulting them. But if the sarrafs had expected that the Porte would indorse their demand to be admitted to the counsels of the church, they were disappointed. For when the imperial edict came (May 19, 1847), it was found to support the patriarch in so far as he had insisted on distinguishing between the civil and the ecclesiastical spheres of his administration by establishing two independent governing bodies in the community, each presided over by the patriarch, the one to be known as the Ecclesiastical Council and the other as the Civil Council. On May 21, 1847, Matthew called a representative assembly of the clergy, magnates, and tradesmen, at the cathedral church, and fourteen clerics, all with one exception from the lower clergy, were in compliance with the edict elected to serve on the Ecclesiastical Council, and twenty representatives, in about equal numbers from the magnates and from the tradesmen, were elected to serve on the Civil Council. On the first day of the following month these two bodies entered upon the discharge of their duties. The opposition of a few influential sarrafs in the end forced Matthew to resign the patriarchate; but when, in October, 1848, he withdrew from public life, he had the satisfaction to see that he had accomplished something in the cause of popular government. The aristocracy had been completely excluded from the ecclesiastical sphere of the national government, and half excluded from the civil sphere.

In 1855 the friction between the old aristocracy and the new democracy was as sharp as ever. The movement for popular freedom needed only one more impulse from the central government to reach its culmination in a written constitution, vesting the entire administrative power of the community, both civil and ecclesiastical, in a representative body chosen by popular vote. That impulse came in the shape of the Hatti-Humayoun of 1856. In this document, which, so far as it concerned the internal affairs of the subject communities of the empire, was as much the product of past events in the Armenian community, as it was the basis of subsequent developments in it, we find the first enunciation of the principle of representative government for the subject communities of Turkey. The following is the passage in the Hatti-Humayoun bearing directly on the internal government of the subject communities of the Ottoman empire:

All the privileges and spiritual immunities granted by my ancestors in the beginning, and at subsequent dates, to all Christian communities or other non-Mussulman persuasions, established in my empire under my protection, shall be confirmed and maintained.

Every Christian or other non-Mussulman community shall be bound, within a fixed period, and with the concurrence of a commission composed as heretofore of members of its own body, to proceed, with my high approbation and under the inspection of my Sublime Porte, to examine into its actual immunities and privileges, and to discuss and submit to my Sublime Porte the reforms required by the progress of civilization and of the age. The powers conceded to the Christian patriarchs and bishops by Sultan Mohammed the Conqueror and his successors shall be made to harmonize with the new position which my generous and beneficent intentions insure to these communities.

The principle of nominating the patriarchs for life, after the revision of the rules of election now in force, shall be exactly carried out, conformably to the tenor of their firmans of investiture.

The patriarchs, metropolitans, archbishops, bishops, and rabbis shall take an oath on their entrance into office, according to a form agreed upon in common by my Sublime Porte and the spiritual heads of the different religious communities. The ecclesiastical dues, of whatever sort or nature they be, shall be abolished, and replaced by fixed revenues for the patriarchs and heads of communities, and by the allocation of allowances and salaries equitably proportioned to the importance of the rank and the dignity of the different members of the clergy.

The property, real or personal, of the different Christian ecclesiastics shall remain intact; the temporal administration of the Christian or other non-Mussulman communities shall, however, be placed under the safeguard of an assembly to be chosen from among the members, both ecclesiastics and laymen, of the said communities.

On the basis of the Hatti-Humayoun a committee appointed by the Civil Council, composed of Odian, Rousinian, Servitschen, Arslanian, and others, made the first draft of the Armenian National Constitution,[1] adopted by the Armenian General Assembly on June 5, 1860. This document, after being revised, was confirmed by imperial edict on March 29, 1863, and went into operation in the same

[1] See Berberian, *Armenian History*, pp. 390 ff.

year.[1]   The National Constitution announces the
following "fundamental principles":

1. Each individual of the nation has obligations toward
the nation, and the nation in its turn has obligations toward
every individual of the nation.   Again, every individual has
rights in his relations with the nation, and the nation in its
relations with the individual.

The nation and its members, therefore, are bound together
by mutual obligations, in such manner that the obligations of
the one are the rights of the other.

2. The duties of the members of the nation require them
to share the expenses entailed by the needs of the nation,
everyone according to the measure of his own ability, willingly

---

[1] The Armenian national constitution was first published
(1863) in two languages—Armenian and Armeno-Turkish.   The
Armenian text was reprinted in 1908.   An English translation
of this document will be found in Lynch, *Armenia*, Vol. II,
pp. 445 ff.

The subject of a constitution for the Armenian community in
Turkey recalls to mind the *Polojenye* or governing statute imposed
upon the catholicate of Etschmiadzin by the emperor Nicholas
in 1836.   Both the constitution and the Polojenye were intended
to regulate and curtail clerical power;   but the former curtailed
that power in favor of the people, while the latter, in favor of the
civil autocrat.   By the terms of the last-named instrument the
Synod of Etschmiadzin is placed under the titular presidency of
the emperor, and its decrees must be submitted to a Russian
procurator resident at Etschmiadzin who examines into their
validity.   The emperor selects all members of the Synod and all
diocesan bishops in Russian territory from nominees of the
catholicos, and the catholicos from nominees of the ecumenical
delegates, lay and clerical in nearly equal numbers, assembled at
Etschmiadzin.   The catholicos may not punish a member of his
synod or suspend any of his bishops without the emperor's consent.   Cf. Lynch, *Armenia*, Vol. I, pp. 233 ff., and Balasanian,
Armenian History, pp. 692 ff.

to undertake the services asked by the nation, and readily to submit to its enactments.

These obligations of the members of the nation are the nation's rights.

3. The duties of the nation require that it look after the moral, intellectual, and material needs of the members of the nation, that it preserve unstained the faith and traditions of the Armenian church, that it promote all learning indispensable to man equally among all classes of children in the nation, both male and female, that it keep the national institutions in a flourishing condition, that it develop the nation's sources of income in all legitimate ways and wisely administer its expenditures, that it ameliorate the lot and insure the future well-being of all persons permanently employed in the service of the nation, that it extend a paternal care over the needy, that it settle with an eye to justice all disputes arising between members of the nation, and, finally, that it labor devotedly for the national advancement.

These obligations of the nation are the rights of the members of the nation.

4. The power appointed to act representatively for the nation and to oversee and enforce the proper fulfilment of these mutual obligations is known as the National Administration, to which, by special edict of the Ottoman government, and under the provisions of this constitution, has been committed the management of the internal affairs of the Armenians of Turkey.

5. The administration, to be national, must be representative.

6. The foundation of representative government is the principle of rights and obligations, or the principle of equity. The authority of such government is derived from the majority of votes, which is the principle of legitimacy.

The national constitution as revised in 1863 vests the highest legislative power in the nation in a representative body meeting biennially, called the General Assembly, composed of 140 representatives as follows: twenty clerics elected by the clergy of the capital, forty lay representatives from the provinces, and eighty from the parish communes of Constantinople and suburbs. The members of the General Assembly are elected by secret ballot and on the rotary system by all Armenians in government employ or engaged in medical, literary, or educational pursuits, and by all males of the community having reached the age of twenty-five years paying a minimum annual tax of 75 piastres ($3) into the central treasury of the community.

Under the provisions of this constitution the General Assembly elects at each stated meeting, and commits the conduct of the spiritual and the temporal interests of the nation into the hands of, two bodies respectively known as the Ecclesiastical Council and the Civil Council. The Ecclesiastical Council is composed of fourteen clerical members, and the Civil Council of twenty laymen. Eligibility to these bodies is not confined to the membership of the General Assembly. These councils in turn act through four boards having supervisory powers, and three committees having administrative powers, namely, the Boards of Education, Finance, Convents, and Justice; and the Committees on the Budget, Wills, and the National Hospital. The first three of the above-named boards are each composed of seven members elected by the Civil Council; the last one, of eight, four clergymen and four laymen, being married and having attained to the age of forty years, elected by a joint meeting of the Ecclesiastical and Civil councils known as the Mixed Council. The boards are subject to the jurisdiction of the two councils separately or conjointly according as the matter in hand is religious, or secular, or both. The Committee on the Budget is composed of seven members, and the Committee on the National Hospital of nine, elected by the Civil Council, and the Committee on Wills of seven, three ecclesiastics and four laymen, elected by the Mixed Council. The transactions of the Committees on the Budget and on Wills are subject to the direct supervision of the Board of Finance, while the Committee on the National Hospital, which is a hospital, old people's home, insane asylum, and orphanage combined, is responsible both to the Board of Finance and the Board of Education. The local officers of each parish commune at the capital are elected by vote of all the males of the parish having reached the age of twenty-five years without regard to taxation, and are made responsible to the Boards of Finance, Education, and Justice.

The patriarch at Constantinople, the chief executive of the nation and the nation's civil representative at the Sublime Porte, must be a bishop of the Armenian church, not under thirty-five years of age, and an Ottoman subject by birth. He is elected by the General Assembly from lists of nominees sub-

mitted by a general synod of the clergy and the
Civil Council, and before entering upon the duties
of his office swears fidelity to the national constitution in the cathedral church of the capital in the
presence of the General Assembly, and receives his
appointment from the Sultan. The patriarch presides over the General Assembly and over both the
Civil and the Ecclesiastical Council.

The administration of the provincial bishoprics is
patterned after the central government. The provincial administration is amenable to the central
government, the diocesan bishops being confirmed
in office by the patriarch upon the approval of the
Mixed Council and therefore being held directly
responsible to the former and indirectly to the latter.[1]

A constitutional form of government in the
Armenian community in Turkey at the beginning
had many obstacles to meet. Sometimes the peremptory orders of the Porte for the enforcement of
the constitution alone saved it from overthrow.

---

[1] The Greek and other older subject communities of the Turkish empire followed close in the tracks of the Armenian community in the race for constitutional freedom, and derived like
benefits with it from the promulgation of the Hatti-Humayoun.
The Protestant community, on the other hand, anticipated the
Armenian in the matter of a constitution by four years. A ten-
tative constitution was drawn up and submitted to a popular
assembly of the Protestant community shortly after the promulgation of the Hatti-Humayoun (May 27, 1856). The Protestant constitution differs from the Armenian in this important
respect, that it takes cognizance of civil matters only, and pro-
hibits the election of a clergyman to the post of civil head of the

At one time the Porte itself suspended it (1866–69), and it was restored only on account of the consequent tumult of the people. By the year 1860 the power of the aristocracy had received its deathblow. But the hierarchy, long accustomed to a more or less autocratic authority, could not easily be induced to relinquish its ancient prerogatives, and long continued to be a drag upon the community's progress in self-government. At the same time the great mass of the people were unenlightened and indifferent toward constitutional government; so that there was some truth in the words of the patriarch Megrditsch Khrimian, late catholicos of all the Armenians, when he said, "Since the people have not a sense of their rights, since they do not apprehend the meaning of law, neither is it necessary for their officials to submit to any constitution." At the capital where public interest in the constitution was greater by far than anywhere else in the empire, during the first

community. It provides for a representative assembly with power to vote on the national budget, to elect the civil head of the community, and to appoint annually from its own membership an executive committee of five having charge of all legal and administrative matters in the community. It may here be added that the internal government of the Protestant civil community was from the first representative. As early as 1851 a measure passed at a popular assembly at Constantinople provided for the election of thirteen representatives at the capital by popular vote to have in charge the affairs of the Protestant community. These thirteen were later empowered in turn to elect the executive committee and the civil head of the community who acted under the committee's direct supervision.

general elections, in 1863, out of a possible 3,658, only 1,899 votes were cast for representatives; and in the first local elections, in that year, where there were no tax qualifications required of voters, the proportion of the number of votes actually cast to the number of electors was scarcely higher. It was evident, then, that with the establishment of the constitution, the work in behalf of popular liberty had only begun, and that a long process of education was now to become necessary to impress the people with a sense of the value and the privilege of the franchise.

But steadily that process went on. The principles and practice of popular government gradually became understood. Like leaven that sooner or later leavens the whole lump, the new ideas of constitutional government permeated the nation, and a generation had not passed before the Armenian community of the Turkish empire had undergone great changes.

The establishment of the Armenian constitution commenced a new era of Armenian history—a new era in education, in literature, in social, ecclesiastical, and political life. No subject race in Turkey during the last half-century made such rapid progress in the several spheres just named as did "the Anglo-Saxons of the East." During the decades immediately following 1860 the Armenians developed a system of public instruction which placed a good common-school education within reach of every Armenian child, male or female, and the best of foreign educational institutions in Turkey began to feel keenly the competition of their higher schools of learning. Their literature departed from its former monkish and ecclesiastical traditions, and for the first time began to give expression to the genius of the people. Their distinctions of class disappeared, and Armenian society recognized no supremacy but that of personal merit and education. The power of their hierarchy commenced to wane, and the preference of their thinkers and reformers was increasingly given to the secular clergy; while their monasteries were more and more made to resume their former position as centers of learning, instead of standing as haunts of idleness, vice, and intrigue. Finally, they developed a new democratic and national spirit, and learned to cherish the principles of a free republic within the absolute monarchy of the Sultan's empire.

Nor do the results of the Armenian constitution for the Armenian community in Turkey exhaust its benefits. The Armenian constitution may be said to have commenced a new era for Turkey as a whole. Sixteen years after the first drafting of it, the experiment in self-government for which it had served as a basis was extended to the whole population of the Turkish empire. True, the Turkish constitution of 1876 was quickly recalled. But it was never forgotten by those who had tasted its advantages. The smoldering fires of revolution at last broke forth again. The Turkish constitution is now restored, and free government in Turkey now promises to be a permanent thing.[1]

[1] See Appendix II. Since 1892 the Armenian constitution was practically a dead letter, owing to the troubles between Abdul Hamid and the Armenian community; but the restoration of the Turkish constitution has brought the Armenian also into recognition again.

APPENDICES

APPENDIX I

THE ARMENIAN CONFESSION

The Armenian Confession, so-called, is substantially that version of the Nicene Creed ascribed to Athanasius. This version consists of original Nicene matter, some matter which appears also in the Constantinopolitan Creed, and some peculiar to itself. Unlike the Constantinopolitan Creed, and like the Nicene proper, it is silent on the procession of the Spirit. The clause in it relating to the reality of the incarnation, which is not found in any ecumenical creed, had its origin in the controversies of the Nicene Age. It combats the teaching of Apollinaris (fourth century) who maintained that the pre-existent Logos took the place of the rational soul in Christ, so that his incarnation did not involve the assumption of that part of human nature. In the following translation of the Armenian Confession, the Nicene matter is printed in roman type, the Constantinopolitan in italics, and the Athanasian and other matter in heavy-faced type, and all matter not found in the Athanasian-Nicene Creed now extant is inclosed in brackets:

We believe in one God, the Father Almighty, the Maker [*of heaven and earth,*] of things visible and things invisible.

And in one Lord Jesus Christ, the Son of God, begotten of [**God**] the Father, the only-begotten, that is to say, of the being ("héouténé") of the Father; God of God, Light of

Light, very God of very God, begotten and not created; himself of the substance ("i-pnoutené") of the Father, by whom all things, visible and invisible, were made in heaven and on earth; who for us men, and for our salvation, came down [*from heaven*] and was incarnate, became man, was born perfectly, *by the Holy Spirit, of Mary the* [Holy] *Virgin,* whereby he assumed body, soul, and mind and all that is in man, in reality and not in appearance. He suffered, *was crucified, buried;* he rose again on the third day, ascended to heaven with the same body, *and sat on the right hand of the Father.* He is to come with the same body [and] *with* [the] *glory* [of the Father], to judge the quick and the dead, *of whose kingdom there is no end.*

And we believe in the Holy Spirit, the uncreated and the perfect, *who spake* in the law and *in the prophets,* and in the gospels, who descended at Jordan, proclaimed him who had been sent (Athanasian: "preached through the apostles"), and dwelt in the saints.

[And] we believe *in* only *one Catholic and Apostolic Church, in one baptism* (Constantinopolitan Creed adds: "for the remission of sins"), in repentance, [in the atonement for] and the remission of sins, [*in the resurrection of the dead,*] in the eternal judgment [of souls and bodies, in the kingdom of heaven, *and in the life everlasting*].

APPENDIX II

THE TURKISH CONSTITUTION RESTORED

In July, 1908, the Sultan's army in Macedonia mutinied under the direction of the executive committee of the revolutionary party known as the Young Turks. Niazi Bey, a brevet-major, was the first to raise the standard of revolt. On July 4, accompanied by eighteen soldiers and about one hundred and fifty civilians, he took refuge in the mountains near Resna. Officers and men from different garrisons rapidly flocked to his standard. The revolt spread throughout the second and third army corps, with headquarters respectively at Adrianople and Salonika.

It was an exciting game between the Sultan and the revolutionists that led up to the restoration of the Turkish constitution of 1876. First came the demand, by telegraph, for the constitution, in the name of the army and the "Committee of Union and Progress." To this initial demand the Sultan responded by ordering Shemsi Pasha, military governor of the vilayet of Monastir, to Resna to put down the mutiny. The revolutionists in turn shot the governor dead as he was taking carriage at Monastir. The Sultan then ordered two divisions from Smyrna to Salonika to suppress the mutiny. These troops landed on the 16th, and were immediately marched to Monastir; but the agents of the committee accompanied them on their journey, and by the time they arrived at their destination they had been completely won over to the revolutionary cause. On July 23 the revolutionists telegraphed their ultimatum to the Sultan, demanding the restoration of the constitution within twenty-four hours, and threatening in case of a refusal on his part to order the second and third army corps, 30,000 strong, to the capital. The Sultan called his council together. The deliberations were long and uncertain. Prudence seemed to urge the Sultan and his advisers to accede to the demands of the revolutionists. Osman Feizi Pasha, the new governor of Monastir, had just been captured by the rebels, and was in the hands of Niazi Bey at Ochrida. The Albanians, gathered on the 22d at Ferizovitsch to the number of between ten and fifteen thousand, had telegraphed to the Sultan their decision to cast in their lot with the revolutionists. But a decision of the Sheikh-ul-Islam, head of the Turkish hierarchy and expounder of the Sacred Law, on the question of using force against the rebels, was what finally inclined the balance in favor of a surrender, and insured a bloodless revolution. This dignitary held that there was not sufficient cause for declaring war against Moslems, and that the right of representation in government accorded to the people in the constitution which the rebels demanded was recognized by the Sacred Law. The Sultan's resources were exhausted. Making a virtue of necessity, on July 24, he issued a firman restoring the constitution and ordering the convocation of Parliament. On the 28th of the same month he took the oath of fidelity to the constitution, and on the first day of August confirmed his promises by imperial iradé.

No revolution could have been more startling. In one day the whole system which had made Abdul Hamid's reign one of the most intolerable oppression was overturned, and the people found themselves enjoying a freedom of which they had not dared dream for years. Espionage and the censorship of the press were at one stroke abolished. Non-Moslems were declared on an equality with Moslems in all the rights and obligations of citizenship. Government by Hamid's camarilla was replaced by a government of the people on December 17, on which date Parliament was opened with a brief speech from the throne, while the revolutionary committee acted as the directing force in the nation's government.[1]

The Sultan, however, was by no means resigned to his defeat at the hands of the Young Turks. The dictatorial methods of the committee, reinforced at times by political assassination, and a disregard on the part of the military officers of the new régime of certain religious scruples of the soldiery, hastened the reactionary movement led by the so-called

[1] On the subject of the foregoing paragraphs, see Buxton, *Turkey in Revolution* (New York, 1909), especially pp. 41–73.

Liberal Union which, while professedly in favor of constitutionalism, was ultra loyal to the Mohammedan traditions. The Sultan was quick to take advantage of the situation. If he was not permitted to declare war against the rebels, he, the Imam or head of the orthodox Mohammedan church, could still incite a counter-mutiny against them in the name of religion. He decided to appeal to the religious fanaticism of soldiery and populace.

On April 13, 1909, the plot was sprung. On that day the garrison at the capital, about 20,000 men, including a battalion of Salonika chasseurs (troops from the very army of the July revolution) detailed for palace guard duty, with the Sultan's gold in their pockets, murdered their Young Turk officers, and, led by non-commissioned officers, marched to the Parliament building. They demanded the resignation of certain members of the cabinet, and of the chairman and three members of the Chamber of Deputies, all Young Turks, and the safeguarding of the Sheriat (Mohammedan laws) and the constitution, both of which they declared to be endangered by the new régime. In the course of the day upward of 250 officers of the army and a number of prominent public men, including the minister of justice and a deputy, were killed. Having terrorized Parliament and the whole city and enforced their demands, and having received from the Sultan an amnesty assuring them that they should not be made to suffer in any wise for the day's acts of violence, the troops gave themselves up to a carnival of shooting.   Numerous casualties resulted from the firing of a million and a half shots into the air that night and the following morning.   On April 14 the mob attacked the office and printing establishment of the revolutionary committee in Constantinople, and destroyed everything in sight.   The damage caused was estimated at over $40,000.   The fall of the Young Turks was as sudden and complete as had been their victory in the preceding July.   Those of their leaders at Constantinople that were not assassinated fled from the city.

The army in Macedonia was the sole hope of the Young Turk cause.   And fortunately it was still loyal to the revolution.   The Young Turks in Macedonia immediately commenced the mobilizing of troops.   From Salonika and Adrianople the constitutionalist forces gradually concentrated upon the capital.   On the evening of April 23, Mahmoud Schefket Pasha having assumed command of the invading forces, the advance guard of the army from Macedonia entered the city, and camped within two miles of the Sultan's palace.   The following morning, about five o'clock, the city was startled by the booming of artillery and the crash of rifle fire.   The battle raged in the streets wherever reactionary troops offered resistance.   In some quarters the reactionaries put up a fierce fight.   But they fought under a disadvantage on account of being without officers.   Their barracks one after another sur-

rendered.   In the engagement over 1,100 men were
killed and wounded on both sides.[1]   By noon the
city was practically in the hands of the constitutionalists.   Shortly after dawn of the 25th the guard
of the Sultan's palace surrendered without fighting.

Had the Constantinople troops offered no resistance to the constitutionalist occupation of the capital,
the Sultan might have stood something of a chance
to keep his throne.   The battle of the 24th, however,
robbed him of his last claim upon the people's
consideration.   On the morning of April 27, Parliament officially propounded the following question
to the Sheikh-ul-Islam:

> What becomes of an Imam who has destroyed certain holy
> writings; who has seized property in contravention to the
> Sheriat; who has committed cruelties in ordering the assassi-
> nation and imprisonment of exiles without any justification
> under the Sheriat; who has squandered the public money;
> who having sworn to govern according to the Sheriat, has
> violated his oath; who by gifts of money has provoked
> internecine bloodshed and civil war, and who no longer is
> recognized in the provinces?

The judgment of the Sheikh was brief and unequivo-
cal: "He must abdicate or be deposed."   Immediately Parliament declared the Sultan deposed.   In
the afternoon of the same day, a salute of one hundred and one guns announced the accession of
Mehemmed V.   At three o'clock the following morn-

[1] The constitutionalists' losses were 97 killed, and 160
wounded; the reactionaries' losses were 297 killed, and 585
wounded.

ing Abdul Hamid was put on board a train and sent to revolutionary headquarters at Salonika, where, as I write these lines (May, 1909), he is held as a prisoner. Constantinople is now under martial law, and many of the instigators of, and participants in, the uprising of April 13 and 14 have already been court-martialed and executed.

The following is a translation of the Turkish constitution, promulgated December 23, 1876:[1]

THE TURKISH CONSTITUTION
THE OTTOMAN EMPIRE

ARTICLE 1. The Ottoman empire, composed of its present provinces, dominions, and autonomous dependencies, being a unit, shall not at any time or for any cause suffer division.

ART. 2. The capital of the Ottoman empire is the city of Constantinople. This city shall not enjoy special privileges and immunities over the other cities of the empire.

ART. 3. The high Ottoman Imperial Office, which includes the high Caliphate of Islam, shall be inherited, according to traditional usage, by the oldest living member of the House of Osman.

ART. 4. His Imperial Majesty shall be by virtue of his Caliphate the Defender of the Islamic Faith, as well as the Sovereign and Emperor of all Ottoman subjects in general.

ART. 5. The Royal person of His Imperial Majesty shall be held sacred and irresponsible.

ART. 6. The freedom, the real and personal property, and

---

[1] I have been unable to secure a copy of the original Turkish or French text. The translation here given is based on two Armenian translations, the one made from the French original, the other, somewhat varying from the first in style and matter, apparently made from the Turkish. It is, however, believed to be substantially correct.

the life-incomes of members of the House of Osman shall be under the guarantee of the Nation.

Art. 7. Among the sacred royal powers of His Imperial Majesty shall be the following: To appoint and dismiss the Cabinet; to confer titles and offices; to bestow decorations; to appoint officers in autonomous provinces according to their charters of autonomy; to coin money; to require the mention of his name in public worship; to make treaties with foreign powers; to declare war and to make peace; to command the military and naval forces; to oversee all military operations; to enforce the Sheriat and other laws; to establish special by-laws for the regulation of the business of government offices; to commute or remit penal sentences; to open and to close the sessions of the General Assembly, and in case of necessity to dissolve the Chamber of Deputies on condition of ordering another election.

Civil Rights of Ottomans

Art. 8. All subjects of the Ottoman empire, of whatever religion or creed, without exception, shall be known as Ottomans. The status of an Ottoman subject shall be secured or forfeited only according to law.

Art. 9. All Ottomans shall be masters of their own personal liberties, on the sole condition that they do not infringe upon the liberties of others.

Art. 10. Personal liberty shall not suffer any manner of violation. No one shall be punished for any cause or in any manner other than those prescribed by law.

Art. 11. The religion of the Ottoman empire is Islam. While acting on this basis, the government, provided that public security and morals are conserved, shall guard the free practice of all religions known in Ottoman lands, and the free enjoyment, as heretofore, of all the religious privileges granted to the various (religious) communities.

Art. 12. The press shall be free within the bounds of the law.

Art. 13. Ottoman subjects shall be permitted, within the bounds of law and usage, to organize all sorts of associations for purposes of commerce, arts, and agriculture.

Art. 14. Individual Ottoman subjects and groups of individuals shall have the right to petition the proper civil authorities with respect to any matter, personal or public, which they may consider as violating law and usage; also in the capacity of plaintiffs to petition the General Assembly complaining of the action of public officials.

Art. 15. Education shall be free. On the sole condition of conformity to the laws in force, any Ottoman subject may conduct either a public or a private course of instruction according to his choice.

Art. 16. All schools shall be subject to the supervision of the government. All proper means shall be employed to secure unity and uniformity in the education of all Ottoman subjects. The religious instruction in the various communities shall continue unaltered.

Art. 17. All Ottoman subjects shall be equal before the law, and, without prejudice to religion and creed, in all the rights and obligations of citizenship.

Art. 18. Ottoman subjects desiring to enter government offices shall know Turkish, the official language of the government.

Art. 19. The government offices shall be filled by men taken from the general body of subjects, according to ability and fitness.

Art. 20. The various taxes shall be levied on all subjects alike, according to law and in proportion to each one's ability.

Art. 21. Each one shall, under the law, enjoy in security the ownership of his own real and personal property. No one's real property shall be taken from him until it shall have been demonstrated that it is indispensable to the public good, and until according to the provisions of the law its proper price shall have been paid in advance.

ART. 22. In the Ottoman empire each one's residence or domicile shall be held inviolable. Outside of circumstances recognized by the law, officers of government shall not for any cause enter by force any one's residence or domicile.

ART. 23. No one shall be forced to submit his case to any court other than the one, under the provisions of laws hereafter to be drawn up, having jurisdiction of the same.

ART. 24. Confiscation, involuntary servitude, and amercement are prohibited. This provision, however, does not contemplate conditions arising from, and taxes lawfully imposed in time of, war.

ART. 25. No moneys shall be exacted from anyone outside of the provisions of the law, under the name of taxes, duties, and the like.

ART. 26. Torture and all forms of cruel chastisement are absolutely and forever prohibited.

The Cabinet

ART. 27. The offices of grand vizier and Sheikh-ul-Islam shall be committed to persons chosen by His Majesty the Emperor. The appointment of the other ministers also shall require the sanction of imperial iradé.

ART. 28. The Cabinet shall meet with the grand vizier as chairman, and shall have in charge the important home and foreign affairs of the country. Those of its decisions which may need special authorization from His Majesty the Emperor shall be put in force by imperial iradé.

Art. 29. Every member of the Cabinet shall attend conformably to regulations to the business pertaining to his own department and therefore coming under his jurisdiction. Such business as may lie outside of his jurisdiction, he shall submit to the grand vizier. In the latter case, if the matter in hand do not require special consultation with the Cabinet, the grand vizier may himself make such disposition of it as he may see fit, or may submit it to His Majesty the Emperor for his decision. Such business as may call for consultation he shall submit to the Cabinet, and shall do whatever may seem to it necessary, in accordance with imperial iradé issued on the subject. The character and classification of these various kinds of business shall be determined by special law.

Art. 30. The ministers shall be held responsible each for the conditions and transactions of his own office.

Art. 31. When one or more members of the Chamber of Deputies shall have charges to prefer against any minister involving matters within the jurisdiction of said Chamber, the course of procedure shall be as follows: First, the question whether said charges shall be brought up before the Chamber shall be referred to a standing committee to whom the president of the Chamber shall send, within three days from receipt, the written copy of said charges. After the hearing of the defendant by this committee, in case a majority shall find the charges in order, the majority report shall be read before the Chamber, and, if necessary, the defendant, either personally or by counsel, shall be heard by it. Then if it is so ordered by a three-fourths vote of the members of the Chamber present, the committee's report recommending a trial shall be sent to the grand vizier, and after the granting of the necessary imperial iradé the case shall be sent up to the Supreme Court.

Art. 32. The method of trial of ministers under impeachment shall be determined by special law.

Art. 33. In cases of a personal and non-official character, ministers shall in no respect be different from other Ottomans. Such cases shall be tried in the proper common courts.

Art. 34. Ministers under indictment of the prosecuting division of the Supreme Court shall be suspended from office until found not guilty.

Art. 35. Whenever there shall arise a difference of opinion between the Cabinet and the Chamber of Deputies over any measure, the Cabinet advocating it and the Chamber of

Deputies positively and repeatedly rejecting it by a majority vote for reasons given in detail, then it shall be the high prerogative of His Majesty the Emperor to dismiss the Cabinet or to dissolve the Chamber of Deputies on condition of a new election within the time prescribed by law.

ART. 36. During the recess of the General Assembly, whenever there shall not be sufficient time to call and convene it to deliberate upon a needed measure, and in case of urgent necessity, the Cabinet shall have the right, in order to relieve the government of an emergency or to guard the public safety, to pass such enactments as shall not be contrary to the provisions of this constitution. These enactments, until measures shall be adopted by the General Assembly met in regular session, shall temporarily have under imperial iradé the force of law.

ART. 37. Any minister may at his pleasure attend the meetings of either house in person, or delegate a subordinate high official in his place; and in the privileges of the floor he shall have the precedence over members of the Assembly.

ART. 38. In the case of a minister being invited by a majority vote of the Chamber of Deputies to submit an explanation of any matter, said minister, either himself personally or through a subordinate high official, shall appear and answer all questions put to him; or, if he see fit, he may, on his own responsibility, postpone an answer.

GOVERNMENT OFFICIALS

ART. 39. All government officials shall be appointed to office according to ability and worth, measured by standards established by law. Officials thus appointed shall not be removed or dismissed until they shall be found guilty of acts requiring a legal removal, or shall offer their resignation, or until the government shall find an absolute cause for dismissal. Officials who shall have served efficiently and faithfully, and officials who shall have been suspended for some necessary cause of government, shall, by special law, receive salaries of promotion, retirement, and suspension.

ART. 40. As the duties of each office shall be determined by special regulations, each official shall be held responsible within the sphere of his own duties.

ART. 41. While each official shall be required to respect the will of his superior, his obedience shall not trespass the limits set by the law.   In acts done in violation of the law, the plea of obedience to a superior shall not relieve one of personal responsibility.

The General Assembly

ART. 42. The General Assembly shall be composed of two separate houses, known respectively as the Senate and the Chamber of Deputies.

ART. 43. The sessions of both houses of the General Assembly shall be convened each year in the beginning of November and shall be opened by imperial iradé, and shall again be closed by imperial iradé in the beginning of the March following.   Neither of these bodies shall be considered as being in session so long as the other shall not be in session.

ART. 44. His Imperial Majesty, when he shall deem it necessary for purposes of government, shall have the power to convene the General Assembly in advance of the regular time, and to abridge or prolong the regular term of its session.

ART. 45. On the day of the opening of the General Assembly, His Imperial Majesty, or, acting for him, the grand vizier, shall be present, and before the ministers and the members of both houses in attendance shall be held the official opening, when an imperial message shall be read dealing with the home affairs and foreign relations of the government for the current year, and with methods and measures deemed necessary for the ensuing year.

ART. 46. Members elected or appointed to the General Assembly shall take an oath promising to be loyal to His

Imperial Majesty and to the fatherland, to uphold the constitution, and to fulfil their duties and to refrain from the opposite; those who shall be present on the day of opening being sworn in in the presence of the grand vizier, and those then absent each at some meeting of his own house in the presence of the chairman of it.

ART. 47. Every member of the General Assembly being free to vote or to express himself as he chooses, he shall not be influenced by another to act contrary to his choice under any manner of promise, threat, or instruction, nor shall he be tried for his vote or for his opinions expressed on the floor of the Assembly, provided that he shall not have acted against the Assembly's own rules of procedure. In case he shall have so acted he may be tried under those rules.

ART. 48. When a member of the General Assembly is charged by a three-fourths vote of the members of his house present with treason or with plotting against the constitution, or with receiving a bribe, or is declared to be worthy of imprisonment or exile, he shall forfeit his membership in that body, and his case shall then be tried and his penalty fixed by the proper court.

ART. 49. Members of the General Assembly shall cast their votes in person, and shall have the right to withhold their votes on any matter under deliberation.

ART. 50. The same person shall not be a member of both houses at one and the same time.

ART. 51. In each house of the General Assembly one more than one-half the total number of members shall constitute a quorum. Questions not requiring a three-fourths vote shall be decided by vote of the majority of the members present. Where the vote is equally divided the chairman shall have two votes.

ART. 52. If any person submit a petition to either house of the General Assembly bearing on some private lawsuit against a government official, and it shall be found that the contents of said petition were not first communicated to said official or to the department to which he belongs, said petition shall be rejected.

ART. 53. The proposing of new laws and amendments to old ones shall belong to the Cabinet. But the Senate and the Chamber of Deputies also shall have the right to ask for the drafting of a new law or of an amendment to an old one, provided that the same shall relate to matters within their province. In exercising this right they shall first seek the approval of His Imperial Majesty through the grand vizier; and upon the imperial iradé being granted, the (legislative) Council of State shall be intrusted with the drafting of the proposed bill on the basis of explanations and specifications furnished by the proper departments.

ART. 54. Bills drafted by the Council of State shall become law upon being submitted to and approved by first the Chamber of Deputies, then the Senate, and confirmed by imperial iradé. Any bill rejected by either house shall not be again brought up for debate during the same year's session of the General Assembly.

ART. 55. No bill shall become law unless it shall first have been read, article by article, and each article of it shall have been separately adopted by a majority vote, and, unless, finally, the bill as a whole shall have been adopted by a majority vote, first in the Chamber of Deputies, then in the Senate

ART. 56. No persons other than ministers or their substitutes, members of the General Assembly, or officers of government officially invited, shall be received or heard in the General Assembly, whether such persons appear in the Assembly as private individuals or as representatives of a group of individuals.

ART. 57. The deliberations of the General Assembly shall be conducted in the Turkish language, and all bills to be submitted for debate shall be printed and distributed among the members prior to the day of debate.

ART. 58. A vote may be taken either by ayes and noes, or by special sign, or by secret ballot. The use of the secret ballot shall depend on the choice of the majority of the members present.

ART. 59. It shall be the duty of the chairman of each house to enforce its rules of procedure.

THE SENATE

ART. 60. The chairman and members of the Senate shall be appointed directly by His Majesty the Emperor. The total number of senators shall not exceed one-third the total number of deputies.

ART. 61. In order to be appointed a member of the Senate one must have won the confidence of the public by some important act, or have gained the public notice by efficient service in the government, and must not be under forty years of age.

ART. 62. Membership in the Senate shall be conferred for life. To it shall be appointed retired ministers, governors, generalissimos, chief justices (*kaziaskiers*), ambassadors and plenipotentiaries, patriarchs and chief rabbis, and naval and military commanders, having the necessary personal qualifications. Members of the Senate seeking and securing government positions shall lose their seats in the Senate.

ART. 63. The monthly salary of a member of the Senate shall be 10,000 piastres ($400). Any member already receiving a salary or other allowance from the public treasury falling below that figure, shall be entitled to the difference only, while a member receiving a similar salary or allowance equal to or exceeding it, shall receive no senator's salary.

ART. 64. It shall be the duty of the Senate to consider the bills sent up by the Chamber of Deputies, and in case it shall find anything in them that it shall consider essentially prejudicial to the religious interests, to the imperial prerogatives of His Majesty the Emperor, to the public liberties, to the principles of the constitution, to the integrity of the empire, to the internal security of the country, to the means for the defense and the protection of the fatherland, or to the public morals, it shall return them to the Chamber of Deputies, with a statement of its views, either rejecting them as a whole or amending or revising them; while it shall indorse the bills approved, and shall send them to the office of the grand vizier. It shall also consider all petitions submitted to the Chamber and if it shall see fit, shall send them to the office of the grand vizier, with its observations.

THE CHAMBER OF DEPUTIES

ART. 65. The Chamber of Deputies shall be composed of members elected on the basis of one for every 50,000 males of the population of the Ottoman empire.

ART. 66. Elections shall be held by secret ballot. The method of election shall be determined by special law.

ART. 67. No person in government employ except a minister shall be eligible to the Chamber of Deputies. If a government official other than a minister is elected deputy, it shall rest with him whether he shall accept or not; but if he accepts, he shall resign his position under the government.

ART. 68. The following classes of persons are not eligible to the Chamber of Deputies: (1) Those who are not Ottoman subjects; (2) Ottomans enjoying under special laws immunities incident to foreign service; (3) those who do not know Turkish; (4) those under thirty years of age; (5) private servants; (6) those who have been adjudged bankrupts, and have not yet had their credit restored; (7) persons of scandalous conduct; (8) those placed under judiciary interdiction as long as said interdiction has not been removed; (9) those who have forfeited their civil rights; (10) Ottomans claiming foreign citizenship. To be eligible at the elections to be held at the expiration of the first term of four years, one must read Turkish, and be able to write it with a fair degree of readiness.

ART. 69. The general election of deputies shall be held

once every four years. A deputy's term of service shall be four years, at the end of which he may be re-elected.

ART. 70. The general election of deputies shall commence at least four months prior to the opening of the Chamber in November.

ART. 71. Each member of the Chamber of Deputies shall act as a representative of the entire Ottoman people and not merely as the representative of his own constituency.

ART. 72. Electors shall elect deputies from the province in which their own district is located.

ART. 73. In case the Chamber of Deputies is dissolved by imperial edict, new deputies shall be elected in time to meet again within six months.

ART. 74. In case a deputy dies, or is placed under judiciary interdiction, or absents himself from the meetings of the Chamber for a long period of time, or tenders his resignation, or is disqualified for membership either by being convicted of some crime or by accepting a government office, another shall be elected in his place in time to serve during the next following session of the Chamber.

ART. 75. Deputies elected to fill vacancies in the Chamber shall serve until the next general elections.

ART. 76. Each deputy shall receive from the public treasury a salary of 20,000 piastres ($800) per year, at the rate of 5,000 piastres ($200) per month, and, in addition, his traveling expenses as provided by the civil-service regulations.

ART. 77. The Chamber of Deputies shall elect by majority vote three persons for the office of president of the Chamber, and three each for the offices of first and second vice-president, nine persons in all, whose names shall be submitted to the Emperor, who shall appoint one from each set of nominees to the offices severally of president, and first and second vice-president, by imperial iradé.

ART. 78. The deliberations of the Chamber of Deputies

shall be public, except when for important reasons the Cabinet, or the chairman or fifteen members of the Chamber shall ask for a secret session, and a majority of the Chamber shall grant the request after voting upon it behind closed doors.

ART. 79. While the Chamber of Deputies is in session, no member shall be arrested for trial so long as the Chamber shall not have found cause for an impeachment by the necessary vote, and so long as he shall not have been charged with a felony or crime.

ART. 80. The Chamber of Deputies shall deliberate on all bills submitted to it, and may adopt, amend, or reject any fiscal or constitutional measures embodied in them. The Chamber shall carefully consider and pronounce upon the public expenditures proposed in the budget, and shall apportion and levy the amounts of the various revenues, in conference with the Cabinet.

COURTS OF JUSTICE

ART. 81. Judges appointed by the government under special laws, and holding an imperial berat, shall not be removed; but their resignations may be accepted. Judges shall be promoted, transferred, retired, and, upon being convicted of crime, removed, according to special laws. Said laws shall lay down the qualifications required of judges and other court officials.

ART. 82. All legal proceedings shall be public, and it shall be permissible to publish judicial decisions. But for certain causes specified in the code courts of justice may hold their sessions behind closed doors.

ART. 83. All individuals shall be permitted to defend their own rights in court by any lawful means.

ART. 84. No court of justice shall refuse to try any case of which it has jurisdiction. Neither shall it defer judgment or suspend a trial after once commencing it or after holding the preliminary proceedings, except when the plaintiff in a civil case shall himself withdraw his suit. In criminal cases the plaintiff's withdrawing his suit shall not stay the prosecution.

Art. 85. Each case shall be tried in the court having jurisdiction thereof. Cases between individuals and the government shall be tried in the common courts.

Art. 86. Courts of justice shall be free from any manner of interference.

Art. 87. Sheriat cases shall be tried before the Sheriat courts, and Nizamié (civil) cases before the Nizamié courts.

Art. 88. The classification of courts of justice, their powers, and the emoluments of judges shall be fixed by law.

Art. 89. It shall be absolutely prohibited to appoint any extraordinary court of justice or any commission with authority to pronounce a verdict, under whatever name, for any special purpose, aside from the regular courts. It shall be permissible, however, to appoint, according to established law, courts of arbitration and referees.

Art. 90. No judge shall assume the duties of judge and of some other salaried officer of government at one and the same time.

Art. 91. For the purpose of defending the public rights in criminal cases, there shall be appointed public prosecutors whose duties and ranks shall be fixed by law.

The Supreme Court

Art. 92. The Supreme Court shall be composed of 30 members, of whom 10 shall be elected by ballot from the Senate, 10 from the Council of State, and 10 from the chairmen and members of the Courts of Cassation and Appeal. The Supreme Court shall meet at the call of the Emperor in the Senate chamber as often as necessary. It shall be the duty of this court to try ministers, the chairman and members of the Court of Cassation, and all persons charged with *lèse majesté* or with plotting against the government.

Art. 93. The Supreme Court shall be resolved into two bodies, namely, the Court of Prosecution and the Court of

Decrees. The Court of Prosecution shall be composed of 9 members elected by ballot by the Supreme Court, 3 of whom shall be members of the Senate, 3 of the Council of State, and 3 of the Courts of Cassation and Appeal.

ART. 94. When the Court of Prosecution finds an indictment, it shall refer the case to the Court of Decrees. A two-thirds vote shall be necessary to the finding of an indictment. The members of the Court of Prosecution shall not serve on the Court of Decrees.

ART. 95. The Court of Decrees shall be composed of 21 members, 7 of whom shall be members of the Senate, 7 of the Council of State, and 7 of the Courts of Cassation and Appeal. This court shall try all cases referred to it by the Court of Prosecution according to law and in final manner. A two-thirds vote shall be necessary in order to conviction. The decisions of this court shall be neither revised nor reversed.

THE BUDGET

ART. 96. No taxes shall be assessed, levied, or collected which shall not have been fixed by law.

ART. 97. The government budget shall give an approximate estimate of all revenues and expenditures, and on the basis of it all taxes shall be assessed, levied, and collected.

ART. 98. The bill of the budget shall be considered in the General Assembly article by article. Accounts containing details of provisional estimates of revenues and expenditures shall be divided into sections after the manner of forms given in the law, and each section shall be considered separately.

ART. 99. In order that the budget may go into effect at the beginning of the ensuing year, the bill shall be submitted to the Chamber of Deputies immediately upon convocation of the General Assembly.

ART. 100. No expenditures outside of the budget shall be allowed from the public funds without special law.

ART. 101. When during the recess of the General Assembly there shall arise an emergency calling for any necessary extraordinary expenditures not provided for by the budget, said expenditures shall be provided for and met by the Cabinet by order of His Majesty the Emperor and under imperial iradé, with the understanding that the responsibility for the same shall be assumed by the Cabinet, and that the account thereof shall be submitted to the General Assembly as soon as it shall have met.

ART. 102. The law of the budget shall remain in force for one year and not longer. But in case under exceptional circumstances the Chamber of Deputies is dissolved without arriving at any decision with reference to the budget, the Cabinet shall have the right, under imperial iradé, to put in force the budget for the preceding year, and to keep it in force until the next following session of the Chamber.

ART. 103. The fiscal report shall show the actual amounts of the revenues and expenditures for the year of enactment, and shall be drawn up after the manner of all financial statements.

ART. 104. The fiscal report shall be submitted to the General Assembly within four years from the expiration of the year for which the budget was adopted.

ART. 105. An auditing committee shall be appointed which shall examine the accounts of all those intrusted with the collecting and disbursing of the public funds, and shall bring in annually to the Chamber of Deputies reports on the same embodying the results of their investigations and observations. This committee shall report quarterly to His Majesty the Emperor, through the Cabinet, on the financial situation.

ART. 106. The auditing committee shall be composed of 12 members, who shall serve, under imperial iradé, during life, unless their removal be required by a majority of the Chamber of Deputies.

ART. 107. The duties of members of the auditing committee and the conditions of their resignation, removal, promotion, and retirement, shall be fixed by special law.

The Provincial Administration

Art. 108. The government of the provinces shall be conducted on principles of decentralization whose details shall be elaborated by special law.

Art. 109. The election of the provincial, district, and cantonal administrative assemblies, and of the general assemblies to be convened annually at the seats of government of the various provinces shall be established on a broader basis than heretofore, to be elaborated by special law.

Art. 110. It shall be the duty of the general assemblies of provinces as will be more fully explained in the said special law, to deliberate on matters of public interest, such as roads, agricultural banks, trades, commerce, agriculture, and public instruction. They shall also have the right to call the attention of the proper authorities to any violations of laws relating to the levying and collecting of taxes and the general administration of the funds, and to demand the correction of the same.

Art. 111. In every canton each community shall have its own council to oversee the administration (1) of all incomes from endowments, whether buildings or other real estate, subject to articles of endowment or common usage, (2) of funds or personal property left by testament for philanthropic or benevolent purposes, and (3) of orphanage funds, which are subject to special regulations. These councils shall be composed of individuals elected by each community according to a special law to be hereafter drawn up, and shall be responsible to the local and provincial assemblies.

Art. 112. The affairs of parish communes in Constantinople and the provinces shall be in charge of parish councils elected by ballot. The organization of these councils, their powers, and the manner of their election shall be determined by special law.

Miscellaneous Provisions

Art. 113. When in any part of the land it shall appear that there is public disturbance, the imperial government shall have the right to declare such a region in a state of siege. This shall mean the temporary suspension of the laws and regulations of the country; and the government of any region in a state of siege shall be appointed by special decree. The banishment from the empire of those who shall have been found, according to information furnished by the Department of Police, to be a menace to the public security, shall rest with His Majesty the Emperor.

ART. 114. Primary instruction shall be compulsory for all Ottoman subjects. Its grades and details shall be determined by special law.

ART. 115. No article of this constitution shall be suspended for any cause or under any pretense.

ART. 116. Whenever it shall be found necessary to amend any of the articles of this constitution to meet new times and conditions, this shall be done in the following manner: The proposed amendment, whether originating in the Cabinet or in either house of the General Assembly, shall first be submitted to the Chamber of Deputies. If it is adopted by the Chamber by a two-thirds vote, it shall be sent up to the Senate. If it is adopted by the Senate also by a two-thirds vote, it shall be submitted to His Majesty the Emperor. Upon granting of the imperial iradé the amendment shall become law. The article of the constitution brought up for amendment shall remain in force unaltered until, after passing both houses of the General Assembly, the amendment receives the sanction of imperial iradé.

ART. 117. Whenever any provision of the law shall require explanation, if of a civil or criminal purport, it shall be referred to the Court of Cassation; if of an administrative purport, to the Council of State; and if of a constitutional purport, to the Senate.

ART. 118. All laws, regulations, and usages now in force shall so continue until amended or abrogated by laws and regulations passed in the future.

Art. 119. The provisional instructions given under date of Shevval 10, A. H. 1293 (October 28, 1876), for the guidance of the General Assembly, shall remain in force only during the first session of the General Assembly, and not longer.

CHRONOLOGICAL TABLE

Dates of Accession	Catholici	Patriarchs	Sultans
August 23, 1808......	....	....	Mahmoud II
September 2, 1809....	Ephraim	....	....
December 27, 1815...	....	Paul	....
November 8, 1823....	....	Garabed	....
September 16, 1831 ..	....	Stephen	....
March 14, 1833......	John	....	....
March 25, 1839......	....	Jacob	....
July 1, 1839.........	....	....	Abdul Medjid
September 27, 1840 ..	....	Stephen (re-stored)	....
October 1, 1841......	....	Theodore	....
June 27, 1843........	Nerses	....	....
July 13, 1844........	....	Matthew	....
October 19, 1848.....	....	Jacob (re-stored)	....
August 23, 1858......	Matthew	....	....
October 19, 1858.....	....	George	....
May 3, 1860.........	....	Sergius	....

BIBLIOGRAPHY

Armenian works are indicated by an asterisk

I. LITERATURE OF THE PERIOD

ANDERSON, RUFUS, *History of the Missions of the American Board of Commissioners for Foreign Missions to the Oriental Churches.* 2 vols. Boston, 1872.

Baptism, An Examination of the Correct Teaching of the Holy Scriptures on. Smyrna, 1845.

*BERBERIAN, AVEDIS, *Armenian History: 1772–1860.* Constantinople, 1871.

Call to Love, A. Paris, 1857.

Constitution and By-Laws for the Internal Government of the Protestant Subjects of Turkey. Constantinople, 1856.

Constitution, Report of the Executive Committee on the National. Constantinople, 1863.

Constitution, The Armenian National. Constantinople, 1908.

Constitution, The National. Second Revision. Constantinople, 1870.

CONYBEARE, FRED. C., *The Key of Truth: A Manual of the Paulician Church of Armenia.* Oxford, 1898.

DWIGHT, H. G. O., *Christianity Revived in the East; or, A Narrative of the Work of God among the Armenians of Turkey.* New York, 1850. The English edition of this work (London, 1854) bears the following title: *Christianity in Turkey: A Narrative of the Protestant Reformation in the Armenian Church.*

EPPLER, CHR. FR., *Geschichte der Gründung der armenisch-evangelischen Gemeinde in Schamachi.* Basel, 1873.

*ERITZIAN, ALEXANDER, *Tonrakian Armenians of Our Day, in Portz.* Tiflis, 1880.

Evangelical Christians, Reply to the First Manifesto Published against the. Smyrna, 1846.

Evangelical Church, Guide for Members of the. Constantinople, 1855.

Evangelical Church, Manifesto and Brief Confession of Faith of the Armenian. Constantinople, 1846.

Evangelicalism among the Armenians, Rise and Progress of. Puragn, Nos. 169–204. Constantinople, 1890–1892.

H., H. A., Reply to the First Pamphlet of the Treatise on the Communion. Smyrna, 1846.

HAMLIN, CYRUS, *Among the Turks.* New York, 1878.

HAMLIN, CYRUS, *My Life and Times.* Boston, 1893.

LANE-POOLE, STANLEY, *The Life of the Right Honorable Stratford Canning, Viscount Stratford de Redcliffe.* 2 vols. London, 1888.

LUCASIAN, H., Protestantism among the Armenians of the Caucasus. Tiflis, 1886.

MEGRIAN, JOHN G., Biography of Mesrop Davidian Taliatian of Erivan. Tiflis, 1886.

MERMRIAN, H. G., The Nineteenth Century and John Deroyentz of Brousa. Constantinople, 1908.

Missionary Herald; Containing the Proceedings of the American Board of Commissioners for Foreign Missions, with a View of Other Benevolent Operations, The. Vols. XVI–LVI. Boston, 1820–1860.

NERGARARIAN, GARABED, *A Brief History of the Beginning of the Mission Work in Nicomedia by the American Board of Foreign Missions.* Waynesboro, Pa., 1885.

New Sectaries, First Manifesto against the. Constantinople, 1846.

New Sectaries, Second Manifesto against the. Constantinople, 1846.

PAPAZIAN, STEPHEN, A Biography of Haroutioun Bezjian. Constantinople, 1864.

PRIME, E. D. G., *Forty Years in the Turkish Empire; or, Memoirs of Rev. William Goodell.* New York, 1876.

SCHAUFFLER, WILLIAM G., *Autobiography of.* New York, 1887.

SMITH, ELI, *Researches of Rev. E. Smith and Rev. H. G. O. Dwight in Armenia.* 2 vols. Boston, 1833.

*TSCHAMOURJIAN, JOHN DER-GARABEDIAN, *An Examination into a Few of the Doctrines of the New Sectaries on Baptism.* Constantinople, 1845.

*TSCHAMOURJIAN, JOHN DER-GARABEDIAN, *Letters on the Communion.* 3 Tracts. Constantinople, 1845, 1846.

II. MISCELLANEOUS WORKS

Armenian Literature, History of. 2 vols. Venice, 1865, 1878.

Armenian Printing from the Beginning to Our Own Time, History of. Venice, 1895.

*BALASANIAN, STEPHEN, *Armenian History.* Tiflis, 1895.

*BALJIAN, ALEXANDER, *History of the Catholic Doctrine among the Armenians, and of Their Union with the Church of Rome at the Council of Florence.* Vienna, 1878.

*BARONIAN, SOUKIAS, *The Council of Chalcedon and the Armenian Church.* Paris, 1902.

BLISS, EDWIN MUNSELL, *The Encyclopaedia of Missions.* New York, 1891. Article "Armenia."

BUCHANAN, CLAUDIUS, *Christian Researches in Asia: With Notices of the Translation of the Scriptures into the Oriental Languages.* New York, 1812.

*CARACASHIAN, A. M., *Critical Armenian History, According to the Latest Historical, Linguistic and Philological Information.* 4 vols. Tiflis, 1895.

*CHAMCHEAN, MICHAEL, *Armenian History.* 3 vols. Venice, 1784, 1785, 1786. John Avdall has an abridged edition of this work in English: *History of Armenia.* 2 vols. Calcutta, 1827.

CREASY, E. S., *History of the Ottoman Turks.* 2 vols. London, 1858. First American ed., in one volume. New York, 1878.

*DER-HOVHANIAN, HAROUTIOUN T., *History of New Juljah at Ispahan.* 2 vols. New Julfah, 1880, 1881.

Encyclopaedia Britannica. Article "Turkey."

GELZER, H., Brief Armenian History. Transl. by Gregory Kalemkiarian. Vienna, 1897.

GELZER, H., *Die Anfänge der armenischen Kirche.* Leipzig, 1895. Armenian translation, by John Torossian, Venice, 1896.

GIBBON, EDWARD, *The History of the Decline and Fall of the Roman Empire.*

GULESERIAN, BABGEN, The Patriarch John Golod. Vienna, 1904.

KALEMKIARIAN, GREGORY, History of Armenian Journalism. Vienna, 1893.

KATERJIAN, JOSEPH. The Symbol of Faith of the Armenian Church. Vienna, 1891.

LANE-POOLE, STANLEY, Assisted by E. J. W. GIBB AND ARTHUR GILMAN, *The Story of Turkey.* New York, 1888.

LEO, Armenian Printing: The Armenians in Modern History. A Historical-Literary Review. Sixteenth and Seventeenth Centuries. Tiflis, 1904.

LEONIAN, GAREGIN JOHN, The Armenian Periodical Press: 1794–1894. Alexandropol, 1895.

LYNCH, H. F. B., *Armenia: Travels and Studies.* 2 vols. London, 1901.

M., H. G., The Olden Days and the Armenian Magnates: 1550–1870. Venice, 1901.

MANTINIAN, STEPHEN, History of the Armenian Church. Valarshabad, 1870.

Mekhitar. Venice, 1901.

MENZIES, SUTHERLAND, *Turkey, Old and New: Historical, Geographical, and Statistical.* London, 1880.

MOURADIAN, M., History of the Holy Apostolic Armenian Church. Jerusalem, 1872.

Panoplist and Missionary Magazine, The. Boston, 1812.

SARGISIAN, BASIL, A Study of the Sect of the Manichaean-Paulician Tonrakians, and the Epistle of Gregory of Narek. Venice, 1893.

*Sargisian, Basil, *Two Hundred Years of Literary Labors and the Noteworthy Laborers of the Mekhitarist Society of Venice.* Venice, 1905.

*Sargisian, Isaac, *Critical Dogmatics.* Constantinople, 1874.

Smith, William, and Henry Wace, *A Dictionary of Christian Biography, Literature, Sects, and Doctrines; During the First Eight Centuries.* London, 1887. Article "Pauliciani."

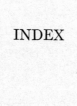

INDEX

INDEX

231

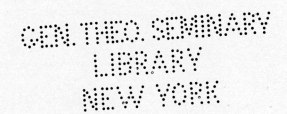